Eyewitness
Electricity

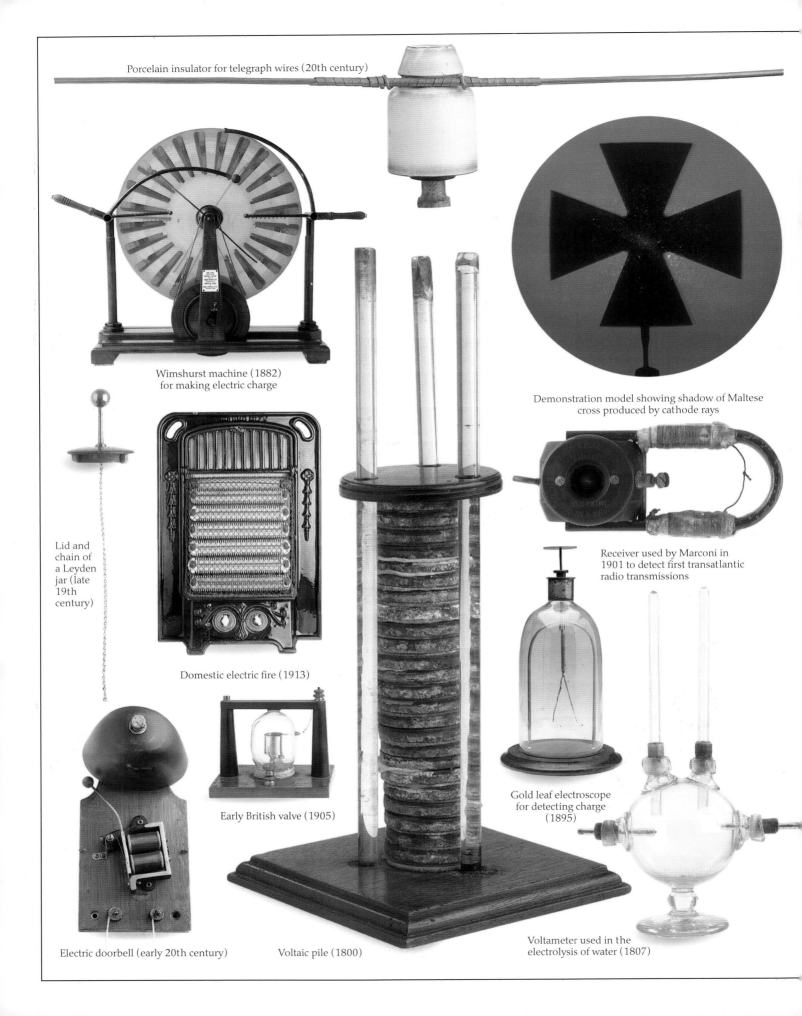

Porcelain insulator for telegraph wires (20th century)

Wimshurst machine (1882)
for making electric charge

Demonstration model showing shadow of Maltese
cross produced by cathode rays

Lid and
chain of
a Leyden
jar (late
19th
century)

Domestic electric fire (1913)

Receiver used by Marconi in
1901 to detect first transatlantic
radio transmissions

Early British valve (1905)

Gold leaf electroscope
for detecting charge
(1895)

Electric doorbell (early 20th century)

Voltaic pile (1800)

Voltameter used in the
electrolysis of water (1807)

Ammeter

Voltmeter

Eyewitness
Electricity

Written by
STEVE PARKER

Tube of pure potassium produced by
electrolysis by Humphry Davy (1807)

Early telegraph cables encased in wood (1837)

Making a wire
glow red hot using
a battery (1895)

DK

Telephone handset (1895)

Penguin
Random
House

Project editor Charyn Jones
Senior art editor Neville Graham
Design assistant Marianna Papachrysanthou
DTP manager Joanna Figg-Latham
Production Eunice Paterson
Managing editor Josephine Buchanan
Special photography Clive Streeter
Editorial onsultant Neil Brown, Science Museum, London

REVISED EDITION
Revised by Steve Parker

DK INDIA
Project editor Shatarupa Chaudhuri
Project art editor Nishesh Batnagar
Assistant editor Priyanka Kharbanda
Art editor Honlung Zach Ragui
DTP designer Tarun Sharma
Picture researcher Sumedha Chopra

DK UK
Senior editor Caroline Stamps
Senior art editor Rachael Grady
Pre-production producers Adam Stoneham, Rachel Ng
Publisher Andrew Macintyre

DK US
US editor Margaret Parrish
Editorial director Nancy Ellwood

First American Edition, 1992
This American Edition, 2013
Published in the United States by DK Publishing
345 Hudson Street, New York, New York 10014

17 10 9 8 7 6
007—187809—July/13

Published in Great Britain by Dorling Kindersley Limited.

A catalog record for this book is available from the Library of Congress.
ISBN: 978-1-4654-0899-0
ISBN: 978-1-4654-0900-3 (Library binding)

DK books are available at special discounts when purchased in bulk for
sales promotions, premiums, fundraising, or educational use. For details, contact:
DK Publishing Special Markets, 345 Hudson Street, New York, New York 10014
SpecialSales@dk.com

Color reproduction by Colourscan, Singapore
Printed and bound in China

Discover more at
www.dk.com

Damaged
lightning
conductor
(1916)

10,000 volt electricity
cable insulated with
waxed paper (1890)

Interior
of carbon
arc lamp
(1870–80)

Pith ball
electrometer
(19th century)

Contents

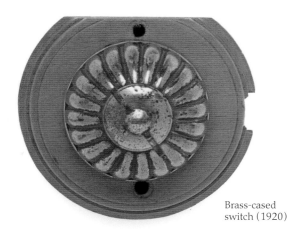

Brass-cased switch (1920)

6
A mysterious force
8
Ideas about electricity
10
The quest for knowledge
12
Collecting electric charge
14
Using charges
16
A flow of charge
18
Electricity from chemicals
20
Circuits and conductors
22
Resisting electricity
24
Measuring and quantifying
26
Magnetism from electricity
28
Electromagnets
30
Electromagnets at work
32
Discoveries using electricity
34
Electricity from magnetism
36
Magneto-electric machines
38
Making things move
40
Manipulating electricity
42
Early electricity supplies

44
The power plant
46
Electricity in the home
48
Electrical appliances
50
Electricity and medicine
52
Heat, pressure, and light
54
Investigating cathode rays
56
Communicating with electricity
58
Talking with electricity
60
Communicating without wires
62
Television
64
Did you know?
66
Life without electricity
68
Find out more
70
Glossary
72
Index

A mysterious force

SINCE THE BEGINNING OF THE UNIVERSE, there has been electricity. Even when there was no life on our planet, more than 4 billion years ago, great bolts of lightning lit up the skies. Lightning is one of nature's most dramatic demonstrations of the energy form we call electricity. As life evolved, electricity became a vital part of the living world. It forms the basis of a nerve signal. Eyes receive light rays and turn them into tiny electrical signals that pass along nerves into the brain and from there to the rest of the body. Our whole awareness and ability to think and move depends on tiny electrical signals whizzing around the nerve pathways inside the brain. In the past few centuries, scientists have gradually begun to unravel the mysteries of electricity. Their advances were often linked to progress in other areas of science. Following this scientific research came exploitation. Inventors used electrical energy to serve our needs (pp. 46–49).

Thales of Miletus

THE VIEWS OF THE ANCIENTS
The Ancient Greeks were among the first thinkers in the scientific tradition. One of the earliest Greek scientists was Thales of Miletus (c. 625–547 BCE), who was a skillful mathematician. None of Thales' own writings survive, but reports of his work show that he is believed to have carried out simple experiments into the effects of what we now call electricity and magnetism.

ATTRACTION
Some of the earliest known scientific experiments were carried out by people such as Thales (below left) in ancient Greece. If a piece of amber (the gum or resin from trees that has fossilized and turned solid) is rubbed briskly with a piece of wool or fur and brought near to a light object such as a feather, the feather flies up and clings to the amber. The word "electricity" comes from *elektron*, the Greek term for amber.

Amber

Feather flies up as though lifted by an invisible hand

Feathers are light enough to be attracted to the amber

Charge is gradually lost, the amber loses its attraction, and the feathers float down

ELECTRICITY IN THE AIR

The lightning bolt is an awesome example of electricity in action. The explanations of what electricity is, where it comes from, and how it works are central to our understanding of matter and the fundamental forces of nature. Lightning is the result of the discharge of an electric charge in a cloud. The energy of the discharge is so great that it produces an intense trail of light, heat, and sound—thunder. It can destroy buildings, kill humans, and consume trees in a sheet of flame. Observations of lightning led scientists and thinkers such as Benjamin Franklin (pp. 8–9) to investigate and begin to unravel the mysteries of electric charge.

PLAYING TRICKS

In times gone by, teachers showed the attraction of magnetic and electrically charged objects, even though they did not understand their nature. Magicians still use the attracting powers of magnetism and "static" electricity (or electric charge) in their acts.

ELECTRICITY IN THE HUMAN BODY

Human life depends on electricity. About every second, tiny electrical signals spread through the heart muscle, triggering and coordinating a heartbeat. These signals send "echoes" through the body tissues to the skin. Here they can be detected by metal sensors and displayed as a wavy line called the electrocardiogram (p. 51).

ELECTRICITY IN ANIMALS

In the animal world, a busy muscle produces small pulses of electricity. Creatures have capitalized on this for hunting and killing. The electric ray has modified muscle blocks on each side of its head. These jellylike "living batteries" send shock waves through the water to stun or kill a nearby victim. A typical shark has 1,000 electricity-sensing pits on its skin, mainly around its head. They pick up tiny electrical pulses from the active muscles of fish. A shark can home in on its meal with complete accuracy even in complete darkness by using its electrical-navigation sensors.

Electricity-producing muscle blocks

Nerves controlling electric organs

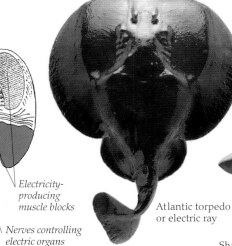

Atlantic torpedo or electric ray

Shark

Ideas about electricity

In the early days of experiments with electricity, scientists had no batteries to make electricity. Instead, they made it themselves by rubbing certain materials together. In about 1600, William Gilbert suggested there were two kinds of electricity, based on the material used for rubbing, although he did not know why this was so. Glass rubbed with silk made vitreous electricity, and amber rubbed with fur made resinous electricity. His experiments showed that objects containing the same kind of electricity repelled each other, while those containing different kinds attracted each other (pp. 10–11). Benjamin Franklin also believed that there were two kinds of electricity. He proposed that electrical charge was like "fluid" spreading itself through an object. It could jump to another object, making a spark.

Versorium

Finely balanced thin pointer of light wood

Upright rod

GILBERT'S VERSORIUM
William Gilbert (1544–1603) was a doctor to Queen Elizabeth I of England. In 1600, he wrote about the mysterious forces of magnetism and electricity in his book *De Magnete* (*On the Magnet*). Gilbert was the first person to use the word "electric," and he invented possibly the earliest electrical instrument, the versorium. Objects like paper and straw, which had an electrical charge when rubbed, made the pointer of the versorium swing toward them. He called these attracting substances "electrics." Those that did not attract the pointer were "nonelectrics."

Tip bent by intense heat

Lightning conductor

DIRECT HIT
A lightning bolt is a giant spark of electric charge jumping from a thunder-cloud to the ground. If lightning hits anything, it burns it. A conductor directs lightning through a copper strip to the ground, leaving the building safe.

A RISKY EXPERIMENT
The lightning experiments of Benjamin Franklin (1706–90) were copied by other investigators. The scientist Georg Richmann in St. Petersburg, Russia, was killed by the electric charge of lightning when he held a wire-tipped pole up high in a storm. The sparks from lightning were in fact similar to those obtained in laboratories.

BENJAMIN FRANKLIN
To "collect" electricity from lightning, Franklin is said to have flown a kite in a thunderstorm. Electricity flowed down the wet line and produced a small spark, showing that lightning bolts were huge electric sparks.

Charge-collecting metal combs

Charge conducted down chains to jars

Leyden jar

Outer metal casing of Leyden jar

Brush touches across disk as part of charge buildup

Discharging spheres

Wimshurst machine (1882)

As the charge builds up, a spark leaps across the small gap

Conductor arms

PRODUCING ELECTRIC CHARGE

For many years, the Wimshurst machine was used to produce electric charge. The machine works by induction (p. 11). Turning the crank handle starts a process involving the metal sectors that are stuck on the outside of two glass disks—one wheel rotates in the opposite direction from the other—and metal combs that point to the disks, but do not actually touch them. This process multiplies small stray electric charge many times. The charge produced is stored in Leyden jars. When enough charge has built up, it jumps between the two discharging spheres, producing a bright spark. The device was developed by James Wimshurst (1832–1903). Wimshurst machines were used to demonstrate making static electricity—as the charge is sometimes called—until at least the 1960s. The largest machine had disks that were 7 ft (2.1 m) in diameter.

James Wimshurst

Metal sectors stuck to outside of both disks

Two contra-rotating glass disks placed close together

Metal combs point to sectors on glass disks and collect charge

Metal ball

Leyden jar being discharged

Discharger rod

Spark

Lid

Glass jar

Outer metal coating

Pulley

Crossed drive belt

Drive belt

Metal ball

Lid

Metal chain

STORING CHARGE

The Leyden jar was an early device scientists used for storing the electric charge they were making. It is named after the place where it was developed in 1746—the University of Leyden in the Netherlands. The electric charge flows down the metal chain to the metal coating inside the jar. It cannot leak away through the glass jar, so it builds up. If the discharger rod is held near the jar (above), the charge leaps from the ball on top, through the discharger to the outer metal coating on the jar—causing a spark. The Leyden jar was an early type of capacitor (pp. 12–13).

Glass jar

Leyden jar

Hand-turned crank handle

Drive pulley

Outer metal coating

Leyden jar with lid and chain

The quest for knowledge

DURING THE 18TH CENTURY, many scientists experimented with electric charge in their laboratories. As yet, there were no practical uses for electricity; what interested scientists was the quest for knowledge. They observed how electric charge could be seen as sparks and how it behaved differently with different substances. Since electricity is invisible, instruments were needed to detect and measure it. Initially, progress was haphazard. There was no way to make a sustained flow of electric charge—that came later from the battery (pp. 16–19). Startling new discoveries were made that are now taken for granted. For instance, in the 1720s, the English scientist Stephen Gray (1666–1736) proposed that any object that touches an "electrified (charged) body will itself become electrified." Charge transferring from one substance to another one that touches it is a process known as electrical conduction.

JOSEPH PRIESTLEY
Before achieving fame as a chemist and the discoverer of oxygen, Priestley (1733–1804) was interested in electricity. In 1767, he published the earliest history of electrical science—*The History and Present State of Electricity*. This was his personal assessment of contemporary studies.

Electrostatic machine

Friction from leather pressing on glass produces electric charge

Electric charge can jump from the metal ball as a spark

Electric charge collected by comb-shaped metal collector

Electric charge can be stored in the Leyden jar

Hand-turned crank causes glass cylinder to revolve

GENERATING ELECTRIC CHARGE
Electrostatic generators, first developed by English experimenter Francis Hauksbee (c. 1660–1713) in 1710, generated larger and larger amounts of electric charge. They were used by scientists experimenting with the nature of electricity, and also in public to produce bigger sparks for amazed audiences. This machine was one of those made by the successful scientific instrument maker George Adams (1750–95).

Horse and rider electrostatic toy

Charge sprays off the end of the point

Vanes spin

Connection to source of charge

Rider and horse go around

MOVING TOYS
Electric charge was used to work this country scene from the mid-19th century. The metal point was connected to a source of charge; the charge "sprayed" off the end of the point and jumped to the vanes, moving them and the model around.

DEMONSTRATION HOUSE
Wooden houses such as the one in this engraving were used to demonstrate how a lightning conductor works. The walls and roof were made to fall apart easily. Hidden inside was a container of gunpowder. Electric charge from an electrostatic generator, representing lightning, would normally be guided down into the ground by a metal lightning conductor. If this was disconnected in the model, the charge created a spark that set off the gunpowder, blowing off the roof so the walls fell flat.

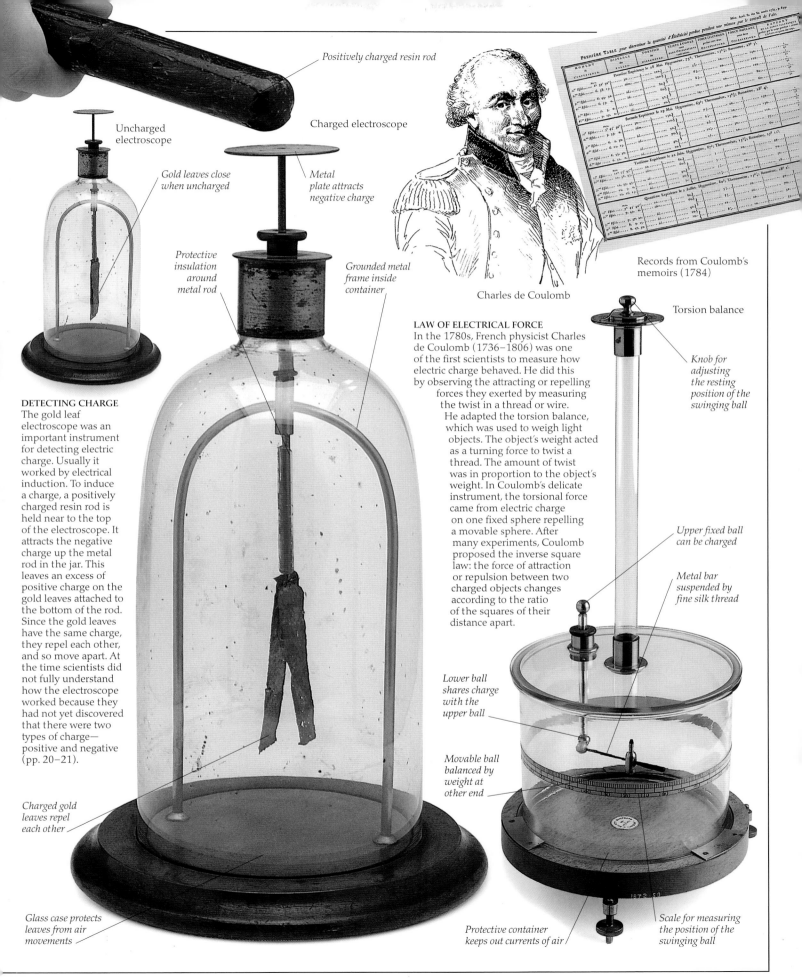

Positively charged resin rod

Uncharged electroscope

Gold leaves close when uncharged

Charged electroscope

Metal plate attracts negative charge

Charles de Coulomb

Protective insulation around metal rod

Grounded metal frame inside container

Torsion balance

Knob for adjusting the resting position of the swinging ball

DETECTING CHARGE

The gold leaf electroscope was an important instrument for detecting electric charge. Usually it worked by electrical induction. To induce a charge, a positively charged resin rod is held near to the top of the electroscope. It attracts the negative charge up the metal rod in the jar. This leaves an excess of positive charge on the gold leaves attached to the bottom of the rod. Since the gold leaves have the same charge, they repel each other, and so move apart. At the time scientists did not fully understand how the electroscope worked because they had not yet discovered that there were two types of charge—positive and negative (pp. 20–21).

LAW OF ELECTRICAL FORCE

In the 1780s, French physicist Charles de Coulomb (1736–1806) was one of the first scientists to measure how electric charge behaved. He did this by observing the attracting or repelling forces they exerted by measuring the twist in a thread or wire. He adapted the torsion balance, which was used to weigh light objects. The object's weight acted as a turning force to twist a thread. The amount of twist was in proportion to the object's weight. In Coulomb's delicate instrument, the torsional force came from electric charge on one fixed sphere repelling a movable sphere. After many experiments, Coulomb proposed the inverse square law: the force of attraction or repulsion between two charged objects changes according to the ratio of the squares of their distance apart.

Upper fixed ball can be charged

Metal bar suspended by fine silk thread

Lower ball shares charge with the upper ball

Movable ball balanced by weight at other end

Charged gold leaves repel each other

Glass case protects leaves from air movements

Protective container keeps out currents of air

Scale for measuring the position of the swinging ball

Collecting electric charge

Today, charge-producing electrostatic generators are an unfamiliar sight, confined to museums and research laboratories. These machines were designed to produce large charges and extremely high voltages. Charge-storing devices are vital components found inside many electrical devices, from washing machines to cell phones. They used to be known as condensers but are now called capacitors. There are many different types of capacitor (opposite), yet they all use the same principle as the Leyden jar (pp. 8–9), the first electrical storage container. Capacitors are among the few electrical devices, such as batteries, that can store electrical charge. They are also used to separate alternating current (a.c.) from direct current (d.c.).

THE SPARK OF LIFE
The electrostatic generator's giant sparks made impressive special effects at the movies. Their similarity to lightning bolts fit neatly into the plot of Mary Shelley's horror story *Frankenstein*. Doctor Frankenstein's monster, made from sewn-together parts of dead bodies, is jolted into life by the shock from a lightning bolt.

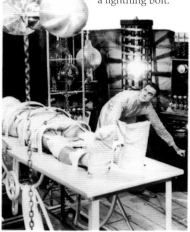

VAN DE GRAAFF GENERATOR
American scientist Robert Van de Graaff (1901–67) developed a machine in the early 1930s for collecting and storing huge amounts of electric charge. He is shown here with one of his smaller electrostatic generators. The charge in the machine, which is named after him, builds up on a metal sphere and reaches an incredible 10 million volts. The machine is mostly used as a research tool for studying the particles that make up atoms. The vast energy represented by its accumulated charge is transferred to the atoms' particles by accelerating the particles to enormous speed so that scientists can study their interactions as they smash together.

Robert Van de Graaff

SPEEDING PARTICLES
The Cockcroft–Walton generator at Brookhaven Laboratory on Long Island, New York, generates electrical energy in the form of ultra-high voltages. The energy speeds up parts of atoms so fast that they travel a distance equivalent to the Moon and back in four seconds.

ACCUMULATING CHARGE
In the Van de Graaff generator (below), the source of positive electric charge is a comb-shaped charge-sprayer connected to the electricity supply. The charge is carried on a moving belt to a charge collector above. This transfers it to the exterior of the large metal sphere. The sphere is mounted on a column that prevents the charge from leaking away. In atomic research there are no sparks; the fast-moving subatomic particles carry the charge away. In public demonstrations, such as this model at the Boston Museum of Science (right), the accumulated charge leaps across to another piece of metal nearby, with a giant spark like a mini lightning bolt.

How the Van de Graaff works

Charge collector

Sphere

Tube in which subatomic particles can be accelerated

Moving belt

Charge-spraying comb

Electricity supply

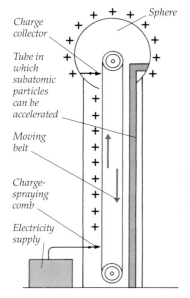

Capacitors

There are many different types of capacitor that store electric charge. Two sheets of metal, or a similar electrical conductor, are separated by an insulating material such as paper or air. In a Leyden jar, the glass of the jar is the separating substance. Capacitance is measured in units called farads after Michael Faraday (pp. 34–35). One farad is a huge amount of charge, and most modern capacitors are fingertip-sized items rated at microfarads (millionths of a farad) or less.

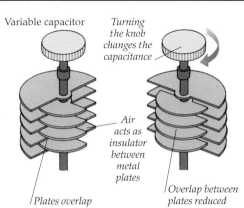

Variable capacitor

Turning the knob changes the capacitance

Air acts as insulator between metal plates

Plates overlap

Overlap between plates reduced

CAPACITORS AT WORK

In electrical devices, a capacitor is used to store charge and release it at a certain moment, or to resist the continuous flow of charge through it. Bigger conducting plates, and a narrower gap between them, increases the amount of charge stored. The tuning knob on this 1950s radio operates a variable capacitor, altering the overlap between its stack of metal plates. This changes the capacitance and causes the radio to respond to signals of a different frequency, that is, to pick up a different radio station.

Metal plates of variable capacitor

Tuning knob

Using charges

THE DUST RESTING on a television screen is an example of electrostatic attraction. The surface of the screen becomes electrically charged while the television is on. It then attracts and holds any floating specks that happen to come near. This phenomenon of electrostatic forces, where there is attraction by unlike charges and repulsion by like ones, is put to work in a variety of modern machines and processes. For instance, in the body-painting shop of a car manufacturer, tiny droplets of spray paint are all given the same electric charge. They repel each other and are attracted toward the car's body, and so settle on it as a more even coating. This is exactly the same principle as the charge that amber, when rubbed, produces to pick up feathers (pp. 6–7).

THE CARLSON COPIER
In 1938, American lawyer Chester Carlson (1906–68) devised a process known as electrophotography. He wanted a machine that could duplicate patent application forms—not only the words, but also complicated drawings. He invented an electrostatic printer, or xerography machine, (from the Greek words *xeros* meaning "dry," and *graphos* for "writing"). The first xerographic print (above) was made by Carlson in 1938, but the first commercial copies were not produced until the 1950s.

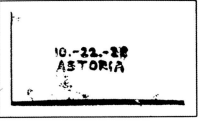

Carlson's first print

Carlson with his early copier

Xerox copier (1960)

Charging chamber with top removed

Outer casing

Selenium-coated plate

Charging wires

Plate-charging button

Edge of selenium-coated plate

Developing tray with toner inside

"DRY WRITING"
The Xerox copier uses the attraction of unlike electric charges (pp. 10–11). At its heart is a special metal plate coated with a substance called selenium. A pattern of positive charges on the plate, representing the black areas to be copied, attracts negatively charged particles of a fine black powder—the toner. (The toner becomes negatively charged by contact with tiny glass beads in the developing tray.) The toner pattern is transferred to a blank sheet of paper and heat-sealed in place. In a modern copier, the selenium-coated plate is on a rotating drum. Otherwise, the process is much the same as this 1960s machine, but now it happens automatically.

Special toner tray (used for copying half-tone pictures)

Making a photocopy

1 CHARGING AND EXPOSING THE PLATE

The selenium-coated plate is put in the charging chamber and, as the electrified wires pass over, it receives an even coating of positive charges. The protective shield is replaced and the plate removed to a camera, where it is exposed to the document to be copied. An image of the document is shone on to it by a camera lens. Where light hits the plate, from the white areas of the original document, the selenium becomes a conductor, and the charge flows away. Where no light reaches, the charge remains.

Plate in charging chamber is positively charged

Light must be kept out until the developing stage is complete

Plate is locked in developing tray

2 DEVELOPING THE PLATE

The plate now has an exact mirror copy of the original document on its surface, in the form of a pattern of positive electrostatic charge. With the protective shield in place, the plate is locked to the developing tray. The shield is removed, and the plate swings backward and forward. As this happens the toner in the developing tray cascades over the plate. Its tiny negatively charged grains are attracted to the positively charged areas of the plate, where they stick.

Selenium-coated plate with toner adhering to it

3 THE DEVELOPED IMAGE

The plate is removed from the developer tray. This reveals the selenium-coated plate with the fine powder adhering to it, as an exact but mirror-image replica of the original document. The plate is returned to the charging chamber.

The plate and paper are slid into the charging chamber

4 POWDER TO PAPER

The next stage also depends on electrostatic attraction. A sheet of blank paper is placed over the plate and its powder image. The plate and paper are pushed back into the charging chamber and withdrawn again while the transfer switch is depressed. The paper becomes positively charged so that it attracts the toner powder away from the plate.

The paper now holds a duplicate of the original

5 REMOVING THE COPY

The paper is carefully lifted from the plate, bringing with it the pattern of toner, which is now stuck to it by electrostatic attraction. The copied parts have been reversed again, so that they are an exact duplicate of the original.

The paper is baked in the fuser

6 HEAT-SEALING THE COPY

Finally, the plain paper with its powder pattern is placed on the fuser tray and pushed into an ovenlike chamber for a few seconds. The powder bakes and melts into the fibers of the paper, permanently sealing the image. The entire process takes about three minutes—much longer than the couple of seconds in a modern photocopier.

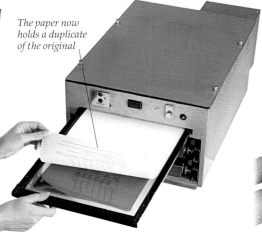

DUST-EATING AIR FILTER

The electrostatic air filter on this 1930s cigarette card, showing a man demonstrating the filter with cigarette smoke, uses a fan to draw in a stream of dusty, impure air. A prefilter traps the bigger floating particles. The remaining small ones pass through the first electrified grid of a device called the electrostatic precipitator. This grid gives each particle a negative charge. The particles are repelled from the negative wires on to the precipitator's second, positively charged grid. They are attracted to it, and stick to its mesh. A filter then absorbs any odors and cleaned air blows out the other end.

How an electrostatic precipitator works

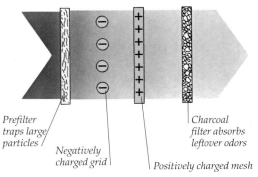

Prefilter traps large particles

Negatively charged grid

Positively charged mesh

Charcoal filter absorbs leftover odors

A flow of charge

In 1780, while Italian anatomist Luigi Galvani (1737–98) was dissecting and studying a frog, he noticed that when his sharp scalpel touched the nerves in the frog's leg, the leg twitched. Galvani suspected that there was electricity in the frog's muscles and experimented to explain what he had seen. Soon, another Italian, Alessandro Volta (1745–1827), heard of the incident. Volta disagreed with Galvani's ideas. He had already developed a device for producing small amounts of electric charge—the electrophorus. In 1800, he announced that he had found a new source of electricity, one that produced electricity continuously (unlike the Leyden jar, which discharged instantly). It became known as the voltaic pile. Galvani thought electricity came from animals' bodies when touched by two metals, calling it "animal electricity." Volta thought it came from contact between metals only; he called it "metallic electricity." Galvani and Volta disagreed strongly, and they and their supporters argued for years. We now know that neither was totally correct.

Galvani's laboratory

Voltaic pile

Glass supporting rod

THE VOLTAIC PILE
This device used two different metals, separated by moist chemicals, to produce a flow of electric charge. The original voltaic pile used three types of disk: zinc, pasteboard or leather, and copper. The pasteboard was soaked in a solution of salt or weak acid such as vinegar. In an electrochemical reaction, the copper loses electrons (p. 20) to the solution and the zinc gains electrons from the solution. At the same time, zinc dissolves and hydrogen gas is produced at the surface of the copper. When the charge flows away along wires, the chemicals separate out more charge. And so electric charge continues to flow. Volta had invented the earliest electric cell. He piled up many of these cells or three-disk units to strengthen the effect. In this way he produced the first battery, which is a collection of cells (pp. 18–19).

Copper disk

Zinc disk

Pasteboard disk

LUIGI GALVANI
Galvani studied the effects of electric charge from Leyden jars and electrostatic machines on animals. In a number of ways, Galvani brought animal tissue into contact with two metals in his laboratory (above). He noticed convulsions in the limbs of the dead animals. Chemicals in the nerves and muscles, when placed between the metals, had caused an electrochemical reaction (pp. 18–19), making an electric cell.

Wooden base

Luigi Galvani

Volta's letter
to the Royal
Society (1800)

Alessandro
Volta

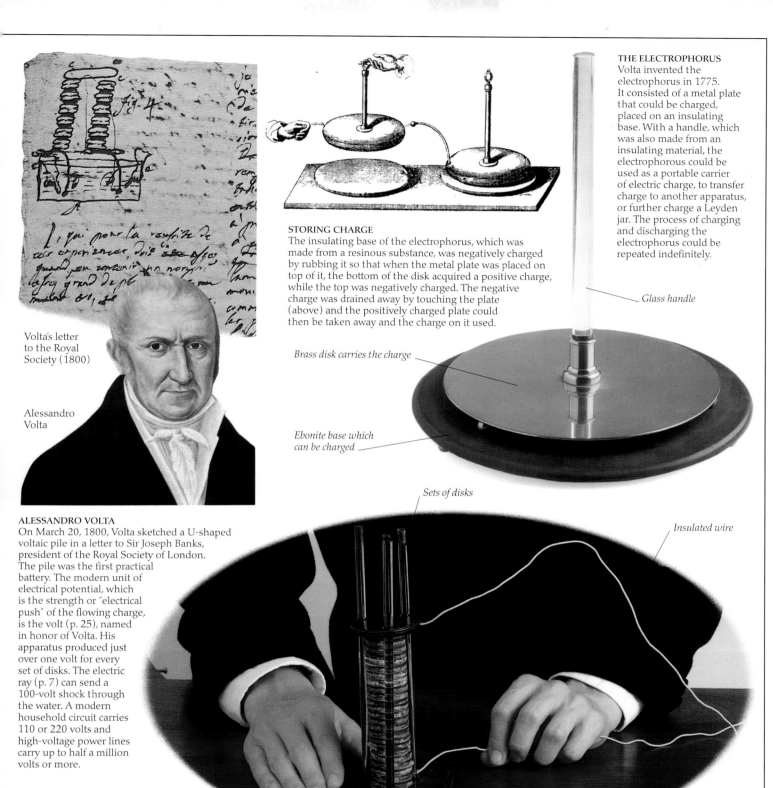

THE ELECTROPHORUS
Volta invented the electrophorus in 1775. It consisted of a metal plate that could be charged, placed on an insulating base. With a handle, which was also made from an insulating material, the electrophorous could be used as a portable carrier of electric charge, to transfer charge to another apparatus, or further charge a Leyden jar. The process of charging and discharging the electrophorus could be repeated indefinitely.

STORING CHARGE
The insulating base of the electrophorus, which was made from a resinous substance, was negatively charged by rubbing it so that when the metal plate was placed on top of it, the bottom of the disk acquired a positive charge, while the top was negatively charged. The negative charge was drained away by touching the plate (above) and the positively charged plate could then be taken away and the charge on it used.

Glass handle

Brass disk carries the charge

Ebonite base which can be charged

Sets of disks

Insulated wire

ALESSANDRO VOLTA
On March 20, 1800, Volta sketched a U-shaped voltaic pile in a letter to Sir Joseph Banks, president of the Royal Society of London. The pile was the first practical battery. The modern unit of electrical potential, which is the strength or "electrical push" of the flowing charge, is the volt (p. 25), named in honor of Volta. His apparatus produced just over one volt for every set of disks. The electric ray (p. 7) can send a 100-volt shock through the water. A modern household circuit carries 110 or 220 volts and high-voltage power lines carry up to half a million volts or more.

Wire inserted under disk

Components of a voltaic cell

Zinc disk

Salt-soaked pasteboard disk

Copper disk

Copper disk

Zinc disk

WIRING UP THE BATTERY
To connect up the voltaic pile to a piece of equipment, two insulated copper wires were attached to sets of disks. With 24 sets of disks this battery produced about 24 volts, which Volta detected with the tip of his tongue on the connecting wires.

Electricity from chemicals

RESEARCHERS FOUND THAT THE SIMPLEST electricity-making unit, or electric cell, was two plates of different metals in a jar filled with liquid. The metal plates are called electrodes. They are conductors through which electricity can enter or leave. The positive electrode is called the anode and the negative electrode is called the cathode. The liquid, which must be able to conduct electricity, is called the electrolyte. Several cells joined together form a battery. There have been many types and sizes of cells and batteries. Some of them used strong acids or other noxious chemicals as the electrolyte. The first batteries supplied electricity for research in the laboratory. Large numbers of batteries were used for electric telegraphs (pp. 56–57). An important advance was the "dry" cell, a development of the Leclanché cell (below), which uses a jellylike paste instead of liquid. More recent advances include alkaline and other long-life cells.

SECONDARY CELLS
Secondary or rechargeable batteries were developed in 1859 by French scientist Gaston Planté (1834–89). In a primary cell, such as a flashlight battery, chemical reactions eventually become spent and no longer produce electricity. In a secondary cell, the reactions can be reversed by electricity from another source. After recharging, the cell produces current again.

Terminal

Zinc rod

Leclanché cell

Carbon rod

Glass jar

Electrolyte in jar— ammonium chloride solution

Central part of Leclanché cell

Terminal

Carbon rod

Manganese dioxide and carbon granules

Zinc cathode

Corrosion-resistant glass container

THE CELL AT WORK
A basic electrical cell has copper and zinc plates immersed in sulfuric acid. When the plates are connected by a conducting wire, chemical reactions occur. Hydrogen gas is given off at the copper plate, which loses electrons (p. 33) to the solution, becoming positively charged. Zinc dissolves from the zinc plate, leaving behind electrons that make the plate negative. The electrons move through the wire from the zinc plate toward the copper. This constitutes the electric current, which continues until the zinc is eaten away or the acid is used up.

LECLANCHE CELL
During the 1860s, French chemist Georges Leclanché (1839–82) devised a cell in which one electrode was a zinc rod and the other was a carbon rod, inside a pot of manganese dioxide and carbon granules. Between was a solution of ammonium chloride. The cell produced about 1.5 volts. It did not contain dangerous acid, and it soon became a popular and relatively portable electricity-maker, and the forerunner of the flashlight battery.

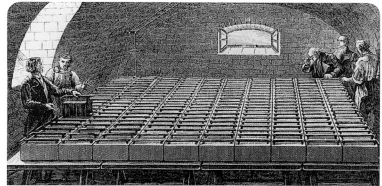

MASSIVE BATTERY
Humphry Davy (1778–1829) was a professor at London's Royal Institution. In 1807, he used a roomful of batteries, some 2,000 cells in all, to make enough electricity to produce pure potassium metal by the process of electrolysis (pp. 32–33).

HIGH-TENSION BATTERY
This 1920s lead-acid storage battery was used to provide electricity for a domestic radio set. "High tension" means that the electricity had a high pressure, that is, a large voltage. Each glass jar contained two lead plates and the electrolyte—dilute sulfuric acid. The battery was recharged at the local garage, where batteries used in the new and popular automobiles were maintained, by being connected to an electricity supply to reverse the chemical reaction. It was then topped off with water to compensate for any water loss through evaporation.

Copper anode

Wire carries electric current

Wooden case

High-tension battery without lid

Glass containers— each one a single cell

Sulfuric acid

Connecting bars

Swinging bar lifts electrodes up when battery not in use

Hydrogen gas

PORTABLE READING LIGHT
A safe, portable battery, combined with the electric lightbulb (pp. 46–47), supplied light wherever it was needed. This late 19th-century train traveler reads with the battery in the bag by his side.

Sealed top-off hole

1940s car battery

Terminal

THE CAR BATTERY
These rechargeable, lead-acid batteries are known as accumulators. Each cell consists of two lead plates, or electrodes, separated by sulfuric acid. As the battery is charged, lead oxide forms on one of the plates, storing the incoming electrical energy in chemical form.

DANIELL CELL
English professor John Daniell (1790–1845) developed a simple cell in 1836 that provided current for a longer period. His cell (right) had a copper cylinder as the positive electrode (anode) in copper sulfate and a zinc rod as the negative electrode (cathode) in sulfuric acid, separated by a porous pot. It produced about one volt and supplied electricity for research.

Sulfuric acid fills void

Cell divider

Lead oxide plate

Lead metal plate

Circuits and conductors

As SCIENTISTS EXPERIMENTED with batteries, they discovered that some substances let electric charge pass through them without difficulty, while others would not. The former were called conductors, and the latter insulators. But why do some substances conduct? It is because all matter is made of atoms. An atom, in turn, is made of particles called electrons (pp. 54–55), orbiting around a central nucleus. Each electron has a negative charge, and the nucleus has balancing positive charges. An electric current occurs when the electrons move. Certain substances, especially metals, have electrons that are not tightly held to their nuclei. These "free electrons" are more mobile, and they can be set in one-way motion easily to produce an electric current.

HENRY CAVENDISH
Forgetful and reclusive, Cavendish (1731–1810) was a great experimenter. His electrical research was wide-ranging, and, like other scientists of the time, he assessed the intensity of electricity by how severely he was shocked by it. One of Cavendish's theories was the idea of electrical potential or voltage to explain how the "push" of the electricity was produced.

INSIDE A CONDUCTOR
Metals are good conductors. In a good conductor, each atom has one or more free electrons. The nucleus cannot hold on to them strongly, and they can move within the conductors. Normally, this happens at random, and there is no overall one-way flow of electrons. But if there is a difference in voltage between one end of the conductor and the other, the negative electrons are attracted to the positive end and so the current flows.

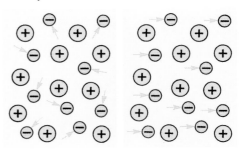

Electrons move at random

Flow of electrons producing current

MAKING A CIRCUIT
A cell or battery on its own does not produce an electric current. Electrons flow only if they have somewhere to go and if a voltage pushes them. When conductors link one terminal of a battery to the other, a current flows. This series of conductors is a circuit. In an open or broken circuit, there is a break along the line, and the current stops. In a closed or complete circuit (right), the electrons flow from the negative side of the battery to the positive side. They can then do work, such as producing light.

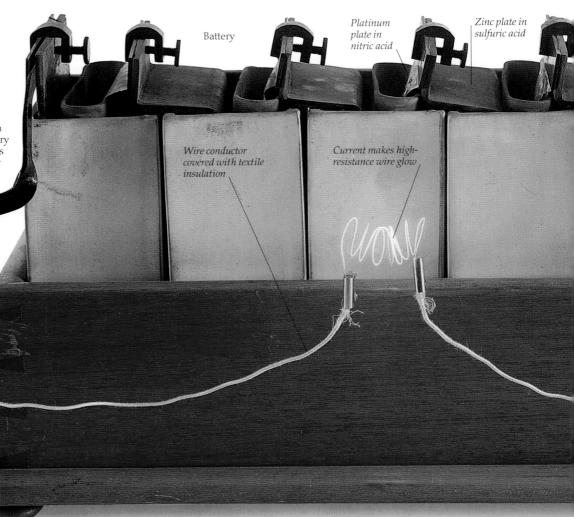

Battery

Platinum plate in nitric acid

Zinc plate in sulfuric acid

Wire conductor covered with textile insulation

Current makes high-resistance wire glow

Open circuit

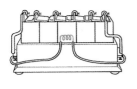

Break in the line

Closed circuit

Carrying current

Early experiments on conductors and insulators showed that most metals were good at carrying current. Soon, wires of iron or, even better, copper and silver were being used in electrical research. Some forms of carbon, such as graphite (the "lead" in a pencil) and charcoal were also conductors (p. 37). So was any watery substance, from solutions of acids and salts, to parts of vegetables and animals. Insulators tended to be woody, fibrous, or made of minerals. An early list of insulators included leather, parchment, ashes, chalk, hair, porcelain, feathers, precious stones, dried vegetables, resin, and amber.

A good conductor

A poor conductor

Charcoal conducts the charge away rapidly

Wool conducts the charge away very slowly

TESTING CONDUCTORS
An electroscope can show whether a substance is a conductor or an insulator. Charged from a Leyden jar or electrostatic generator, its two gold leaves repel each other and move apart. Then the test substance is held in the hand, against the metal cap. If the substance is a good conductor, it conducts the charge away from the electroscope, to the body and then into the ground. The leaves lose their charge and flop back down. The speed with which they come to rest together show how fast their charge is conducted away, and so indicates the efficiency of the conductor.

Gold leaves lose their charge and close together

Porous pot

Gold leaves keep their charge and repel each other

INSULATING PLUGS
For safety's sake, the outside of a plug must be well insulated from the conducting metal prongs inside. Bodies of early plugs were made of wood and porcelain. Bakelite, a synthetic resin and a good insulator, came into use in the 1910s.

Bakelite body (1930)

Wooden body (1915)

Porcelain body (1920)

WEATHERPROOF INSULATION
High-voltage power lines must be well insulated or the electricity may force its way through a poor insulator or spark across a gap. Porous materials, such as wood, are not used because they can absorb moisture. Nonporous substances, such as ceramics and glass, are shaped to keep rain, dew, and other moisture from creating a circuit into the ground.

20th-century porcelain insulator for telegraph wires

Ceramic insulator (1956)

Toughened glass suspension insulator (1956)

Aluminum power line

Resisting electricity

IN A SERIES OF EXPERIMENTS around 1825, the German scientist Georg Ohm (1789–1854) demonstrated that there were no perfect electrical conductors. Each type of substance, even the best metals, put up some resistance to the current. Ohm showed that a long wire had more resistance than a short one of the same metal, and thin wires had more resistance than fat ones. Also, in a circuit, the greater the resistance, the more potential difference (volts) was needed to push the current through the wire. The relationships between potential difference, current, and resistance became known as Ohm's law.

ADJUSTABLE RESISTANCE

Scientists needing to vary the current in a circuit developed adjustable resistors, or rheostats. (These were once used in dimmer switches.) One simple design used special resistance wire, made from a combination of metals such as nickel and copper. Resistance wire put up some resistance to the current, but not too much. A long piece of the resistance wire was wound as a coil on an insulating tube. This was more convenient than having it stretched out straight. The wire touched a contact that slid along the top. Electricity from a battery came in through one terminal, then into the resistance coil. As the contact slid one way, the electricity went through more resistance wire, so the rheostat's resistance rose. As the contact moved the other way, its resistance fell.

Ammeter shows larger current

Sliding contact is a short distance along the tube

Rheostat

Wire to battery

Wire connecting rheostat to battery

Ammeter

Insulating tube

1 LOWER RESISTANCE
Electricity passes through only a short length of resistance wire, then through the top bar to the red wire. The circuit has a low overall resistance, so a large current flows, as shown on the meter.

Ammeter shows smaller current

Sliding contact halfway along tube

2 HIGHER RESISTANCE
The electricity now flows through more resistance wire. (The bar and other wires give very little resistance.) The circuit has a higher overall resistance, so a smaller current flows, as shown on the meter.

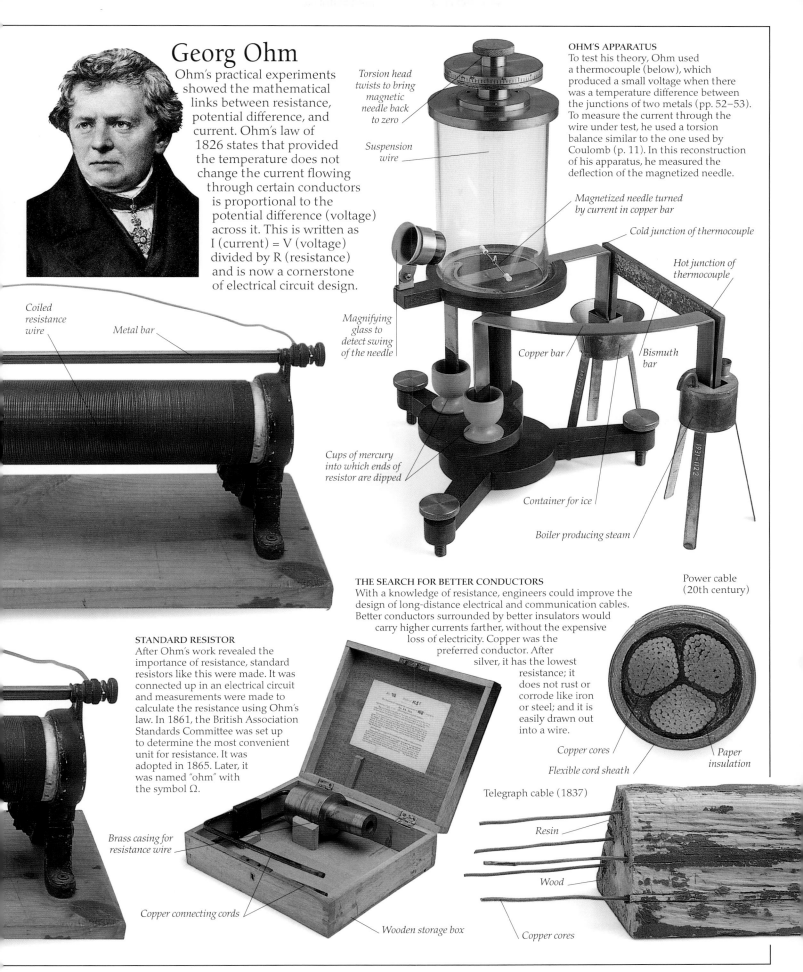

Georg Ohm

Ohm's practical experiments showed the mathematical links between resistance, potential difference, and current. Ohm's law of 1826 states that provided the temperature does not change the current flowing through certain conductors is proportional to the potential difference (voltage) across it. This is written as I (current) = V (voltage) divided by R (resistance) and is now a cornerstone of electrical circuit design.

Torsion head twists to bring magnetic needle back to zero

Suspension wire

OHM'S APPARATUS
To test his theory, Ohm used a thermocouple (below), which produced a small voltage when there was a temperature difference between the junctions of two metals (pp. 52–53). To measure the current through the wire under test, he used a torsion balance similar to the one used by Coulomb (p. 11). In this reconstruction of his apparatus, he measured the deflection of the magnetized needle.

Magnetized needle turned by current in copper bar

Cold junction of thermocouple

Hot junction of thermocouple

Coiled resistance wire

Metal bar

Magnifying glass to detect swing of the needle

Copper bar

Bismuth bar

Cups of mercury into which ends of resistor are dipped

Container for ice

Boiler producing steam

THE SEARCH FOR BETTER CONDUCTORS
With a knowledge of resistance, engineers could improve the design of long-distance electrical and communication cables. Better conductors surrounded by better insulators would carry higher currents farther, without the expensive loss of electricity. Copper was the preferred conductor. After silver, it has the lowest resistance; it does not rust or corrode like iron or steel; and it is easily drawn out into a wire.

Power cable (20th century)

STANDARD RESISTOR
After Ohm's work revealed the importance of resistance, standard resistors like this were made. It was connected up in an electrical circuit and measurements were made to calculate the resistance using Ohm's law. In 1861, the British Association Standards Committee was set up to determine the most convenient unit for resistance. It was adopted in 1865. Later, it was named "ohm" with the symbol Ω.

Copper cores

Paper insulation

Flexible cord sheath

Telegraph cable (1837)

Brass casing for resistance wire

Resin

Wood

Copper connecting cords

Wooden storage box

Copper cores

Measuring and quantifying

In the middle of the 19th century, scientists were busy studying electricity and its effects. They experimented with new types of cells and batteries and with circuits containing different components. There was still no widespread commercial use for electricity, except for the telegraph (pp. 56–57). As with all scientific research, the experimenters had to find ways of measuring, recording, and checking their work. New measuring devices were needed and meters of ingenious design were used by the researchers who struggled to understand this mysterious "force." To make measuring devices useful, new units were devised and named. The existing units, such as yards and meters, were no use for the flowing charge of an electric current.

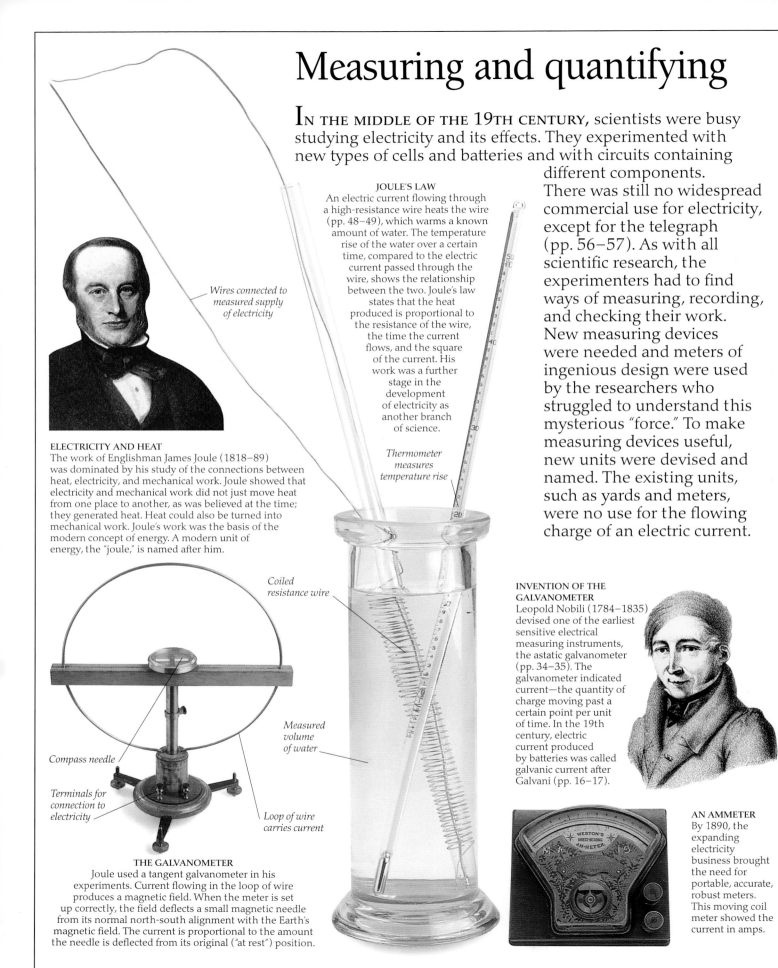

Wires connected to measured supply of electricity

ELECTRICITY AND HEAT
The work of Englishman James Joule (1818–89) was dominated by his study of the connections between heat, electricity, and mechanical work. Joule showed that electricity and mechanical work did not just move heat from one place to another, as was believed at the time; they generated heat. Heat could also be turned into mechanical work. Joule's work was the basis of the modern concept of energy. A modern unit of energy, the "joule," is named after him.

JOULE'S LAW
An electric current flowing through a high-resistance wire heats the wire (pp. 48–49), which warms a known amount of water. The temperature rise of the water over a certain time, compared to the electric current passed through the wire, shows the relationship between the two. Joule's law states that the heat produced is proportional to the resistance of the wire, the time the current flows, and the square of the current. His work was a further stage in the development of electricity as another branch of science.

Thermometer measures temperature rise

Coiled resistance wire

Measured volume of water

Compass needle

Terminals for connection to electricity

Loop of wire carries current

THE GALVANOMETER
Joule used a tangent galvanometer in his experiments. Current flowing in the loop of wire produces a magnetic field. When the meter is set up correctly, the field deflects a small magnetic needle from its normal north-south alignment with the Earth's magnetic field. The current is proportional to the amount the needle is deflected from its original ("at rest") position.

INVENTION OF THE GALVANOMETER
Leopold Nobili (1784–1835) devised one of the earliest sensitive electrical measuring instruments, the astatic galvanometer (pp. 34–35). The galvanometer indicated current—the quantity of charge moving past a certain point per unit of time. In the 19th century, electric current produced by batteries was called galvanic current after Galvani (pp. 16–17).

AN AMMETER
By 1890, the expanding electricity business brought the need for portable, accurate, robust meters. This moving coil meter showed the current in amps.

Flowing currents

Electricity has been likened to a fluid, flowing unseen from place to place. Some of the words used to describe electricity, such as "current" and "flow," relate to these notions. The comparison between electricity passing along wires and water flowing through pipes is not an exact parallel, but it can help to explain some of electricity's stranger properties by making them more physical and familiar.

WATER ANALOGY

The rate of water flow (the volume passing a certain point in a given time) is similar to the current in an electrical circuit, measured in amps. The pressure, or pushing force, of the water can be thought of as the potential difference in an electrical circuit, measured in volts. A narrower pipe resists water flow, just as thin wire in a circuit resists the flow of electricity.

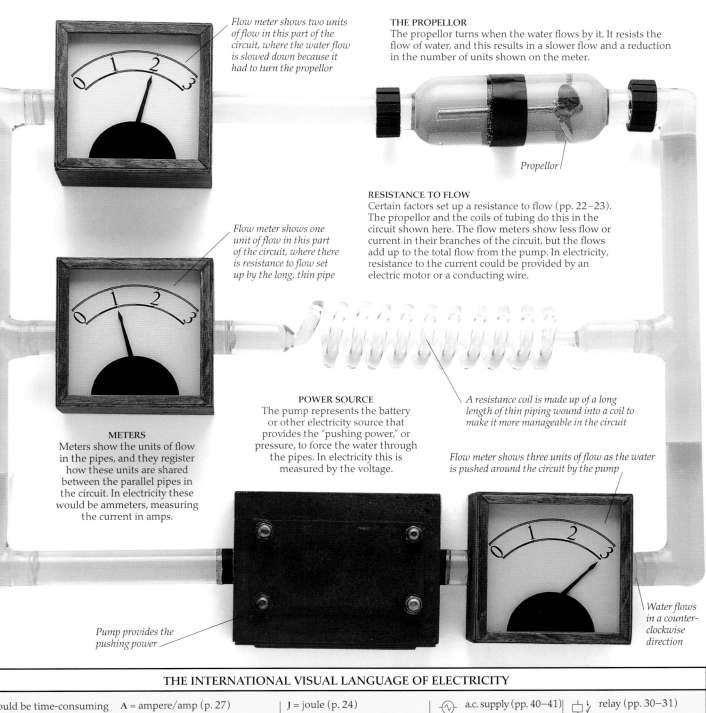

Flow meter shows two units of flow in this part of the circuit, where the water flow is slowed down because it had to turn the propellor

THE PROPELLOR

The propellor turns when the water flows by it. It resists the flow of water, and this results in a slower flow and a reduction in the number of units shown on the meter.

Propellor

Flow meter shows one unit of flow in this part of the circuit, where there is resistance to flow set up by the long, thin pipe

RESISTANCE TO FLOW

Certain factors set up a resistance to flow (pp. 22–23). The propellor and the coils of tubing do this in the circuit shown here. The flow meters show less flow or current in their branches of the circuit, but the flows add up to the total flow from the pump. In electricity, resistance to the current could be provided by an electric motor or a conducting wire.

A resistance coil is made up of a long length of thin piping wound into a coil to make it more manageable in the circuit

METERS

Meters show the units of flow in the pipes, and they register how these units are shared between the parallel pipes in the circuit. In electricity these would be ammeters, measuring the current in amps.

POWER SOURCE

The pump represents the battery or other electricity source that provides the "pushing power," or pressure, to force the water through the pipes. In electricity this is measured by the voltage.

Flow meter shows three units of flow as the water is pushed around the circuit by the pump

Pump provides the pushing power

Water flows in a counter-clockwise direction

THE INTERNATIONAL VISUAL LANGUAGE OF ELECTRICITY

It would be time-consuming if all the information about electricity were written out in full. So symbols are used as an international visual language that is understood by electrical engineers, circuit designers, and teachers.

A = ampere/amp (p. 27)
a.c. = alternating current (pp. 40–41)
C = coulomb (p. 11)
d.c. = direct current (pp. 40–41)
e.m.f. = electromotive force (pp. 34–35)
F = farad (p. 13)
H = henry (p. 35)

J = joule (p. 24)
kWh = kilowatt-hour (p. 46)
p.d. = potential difference (p. 22)
V = volt (pp. 20–21)
W = watt (p. 42)
Ω = ohm (pp. 22–23)

a.c. supply (pp. 40–41)
ammeter (pp. 22–23)
battery (pp. 18–19)
cell (pp. 16–19)
fuse (p. 48)

relay (pp. 30–31)
resistor (pp. 22–23)
switch (pp. 46–49)
transformer (pp. 40–41)
voltmeter

Magnetism from electricity

W**ITH THE DEVELOPMENT OF** V**OLTA'S BATTERY IN** 1800, scientists had a source of steadily flowing electric current. This opened up new fields of research. Twenty years later, an observation by Hans Christian Oersted (1777–1851) from Copenhagen began to link the two great scientific mysteries of the age: electricity and magnetism. Oersted noticed that a metal wire carrying a current affected a magnetic compass needle that was brought near to it. This revelation, which contradicted orthodox philosophy of the time, was published in scientific journals. French scientific thinker André-Marie Ampère (1775–1836) heard about Oersted's work from a fellow scientist. He doubted it at first, so he repeated the tests, but had similar results. Ampère therefore set to work describing the effect more fully and explaining the connection between electricity and magnetism. In repeating the experiments, he provided a theoretical and mathematical description of the practical results of Oersted's work. From this flowed discoveries such as the electromagnet (pp. 28–29) and the telegraph receiver (pp. 56–57).

OERSTED'S ANNOUNCEMENT
Oersted published his discovery of the interaction between electricity and magnetism on July 21, 1820. The pamphlet was written in Latin but was translated into various languages, including his own, Danish. Michael Faraday (pp. 34–35) would probably have heard about the discovery this way.

Current off

With no current in the wire, the filings lie haphazardly

Current on

THE MAGNETIC FIELD
Magnetism, like electricity, is invisible—but its effects can be seen. Iron-containing substances such as iron filings are attracted to an ordinary bar magnet, and they line up to indicate the direction of the invisible "lines of force" of the magnetic field. An electric current also creates a magnetic field. With no current in the wire, the filings lie randomly on the cardboard. Switch on the current, tap the cardboard, and the filings line up to reveal a circular magnetic field around the wire.

Filings line up to indicate circular magnetic field

Trough battery

Battery terminal

Wooden clamp

Current-carrying wire

Dilute acid between plates

AMPERE'S ACHIEVEMENT

Ampère developed the science of electrodynamics. He proved that the strength of the magnetic field around a wire, shown by the amount of the compass needle's deflection, rises with increasing current and decreases with the distance away from the wire. Ampère extended Oersted's work, but he could not see a clear relationship between the needle's movements and the position of the wire. Then he realized that the direction in which the needle settled depended on the Earth's magnetic field as well as the magnetic field produced by the current. He devised a way of neutralizing the Earth's magnetic field and found that the needle then settled in the direction of the magnetic field produced by the current and not with the Earth's north-south magnetic field. Ampère also found that two parallel electric currents had an effect on each other. If the currents run in the same direction, they attract each other; if they run in opposite directions, they repel each other. To commemorate Ampère's achievements, the modern unit of current—the ampere (shortened to "amp")—was named after him.

André-Marie Ampère

Thumb points in the direction of movement

First finger points in the direction of the magnetic field

Second finger indicates flow of current

THE LEFT-HAND RULE

When an electric current crosses a magnetic field, then the magnetic field, the current, and the force on the current—and thus the movement of the wire carrying the current, if it can move (pp. 38–39)—are all in different directions. A current-carrying wire or other conductor in a magnetic field tries to move according to this handy rule. With the thumb and first two fingers of the left hand at right angles to each other, the first finger shows the direction of the magnetic field (points from the north pole to the south pole of the magnet); the second finger shows the flow of the electric current (points from positive to negative); and the thumb shows the movement of the wire.

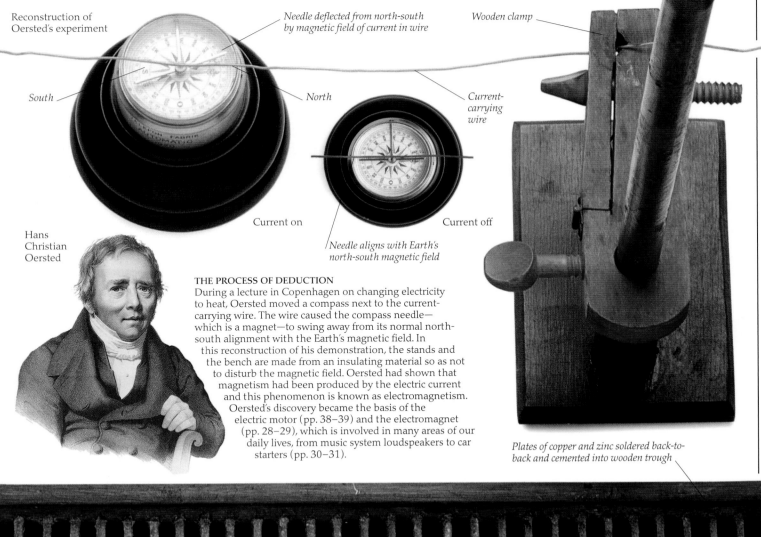

Reconstruction of Oersted's experiment

Needle deflected from north-south by magnetic field of current in wire

Wooden clamp

South

North

Current-carrying wire

Current on

Current off

Needle aligns with Earth's north-south magnetic field

Hans Christian Oersted

THE PROCESS OF DEDUCTION

During a lecture in Copenhagen on changing electricity to heat, Oersted moved a compass next to the current-carrying wire. The wire caused the compass needle—which is a magnet—to swing away from its normal north-south alignment with the Earth's magnetic field. In this reconstruction of his demonstration, the stands and the bench are made from an insulating material so as not to disturb the magnetic field. Oersted had shown that magnetism had been produced by the electric current and this phenomenon is known as electromagnetism. Oersted's discovery became the basis of the electric motor (pp. 38–39) and the electromagnet (pp. 28–29), which is involved in many areas of our daily lives, from music system loudspeakers to car starters (pp. 30–31).

Plates of copper and zinc soldered back-to-back and cemented into wooden trough

Electromagnets

THE DISCOVERY OF a magnetic field around a current-carrying wire (pp. 26–27), and the fact that a coil of wire had a greater magnetic effect than a single turn, led to a fascinating new gadget that made lecture audiences gasp with surprise. In 1825, William Sturgeon (1783–1850) wound a coil of wire around an iron rod and built one of the first electromagnets. An electromagnet differs from the usual permanent magnet—its magnetism can be turned on and off.

It usually consists of insulated electrical wire wound around a piece of iron, known as the core. Switch on the current, and the magnetic field around the wire makes the core behave as a magnet. It attracts iron-containing substances in the usual way. Switch off the electricity, and the magnetism disappears. Sturgeon built the electromagnets as demonstration models for his lectures.

ELECTROMAGNETIC CHAIR
A chair was a convenient base for this great horseshoe electromagnet of Michael Faraday (pp. 34–35). It was used to investigate the effects of magnetism.

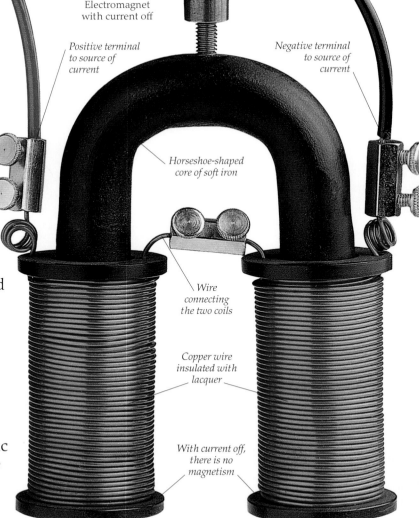

Electromagnet with current off

Positive terminal to source of current

Negative terminal to source of current

Horseshoe-shaped core of soft iron

Wire connecting the two coils

Copper wire insulated with lacquer

With current off, there is no magnetism

Fabric insulation on iron core

Coil of wire

Sturgeon's electromagnet

Iron core

End connected to battery

End connected to battery

STURGEON'S ELECTROMAGNET
Sturgeon was a craftsman and instrument maker who published catalogs of his electromagnetic apparatus (left). He enjoyed the practical "how-to" side of science, but had less concern for theories about why things happened. His electromagnet (above) depended on current passing through a coil of wire to create an appreciable magnetic field. In his time, wires were made bare and uninsulated. He insulated the iron core to stop the electricity from passing straight along it instead. (Later electromagnets had insulated wire.) The turns of the coil were also spaced apart, to prevent the current from jumping straight from one to the next where they touched—short-circuiting.

INVISIBLE LIFTING POWER
This modern electromagnet demonstrates its strength by attracting a loose pile of iron filings when the current is switched on. In a bar-shaped electromagnet, one end of the core becomes the north pole and the other is the south pole, depending on the current's direction of flow. This horseshoe-shaped core has two coils for a stronger magnetic field between its ends (bringing the poles closer together makes the magnet more powerful). Sturgeon made an initial discovery that soft iron was a good metal for the core, since it became magnetized more easily than steel. In the early days, there were races to build the biggest electromagnets and lift the heaviest weights. By the late 1820s, electromagnets in Europe could lift around 11 lb (5 kg). In the United States, Joseph Henry realized that more turns in the coil produced a stronger magnetic field (up to a limit). It is said that he made insulated wire by wrapping bare wire with strips of silk from his wife's clothes. He could then pack more turns of wire into a smaller space, without the risk of a short-circuit. The greater the current, the more powerful was the magnetic field. Henry's "Albany" electromagnet (opposite) lifted about 750 lb (340 kg).

Iron filings

Electromagnet with current on

Positive terminal to source of current

Negative terminal to source of current

Horseshoe-shaped core of soft iron

Wire connecting the two coils

Copper wire insulated with lacquer

Force of magnetic field overcomes gravity and lifts iron filings

Henry's electromagnet

Non-magnetic stand

Iron core

Several layers of insulated wire

Zinc plate

Copper plate

Wooden base

JOSEPH HENRY
Henry (1797–1878) was an engineer whose inventive genius led him to improve electromagnets, for example, by wrapping a second coil of wire around the first. In this small electromagnet (left), the two metal plates of copper and zinc were immersed in a jar of dilute acid. This formed a voltaic cell (pp. 16–17) that produced the electric current. The wire was wrapped in insulating fabric so that the coil's turns could be close together for a stronger magnetic field. Henry also developed an early form of telegraph in 1831, although others made fame and fortune from it (pp. 56–57), and some of his work with electromagnetic induction paralleled that of Faraday.

HENRY'S LIFTING RIG
This type of apparatus was used to measure the lifting power of electromagnets made to different designs, from various metals and with different numbers and arrangements of windings.

ELECTROMAGNETS AT WORK
The lifting power of modern electromagnets is used to separate iron-containing, or ferrous, metals from other materials at the scrapyard before recycling.

Electromagnets at work

SINCE THE TIME OF STURGEON AND HENRY, electromagnets have been central components in electrical machines. Their power to attract and hold iron-containing materials, for example, when sorting out steel cans from aluminum ones at the recycling center, is not their only use. An electromagnet is a convenient way of turning electrical energy into rotary motion, using the forces of magnetic attraction and repulsion in electric motors (pp. 38–39). The reverse occurs in generators (pp. 36–37). Electricity is converted into push-pull movements by electromagnetic relays and solenoids. The movements operate mechanical devices, such as telegraph receivers. Electro-magnetism is also used in electrical transformers (pp. 40–41) and to manipulate atoms in particle accelerators.

(pp. 38–39) (pp. 36–37) (pp. 40–41)

SAVING SIGHT
A finely controlled electromagnet could remove iron-containing foreign particles from the tissues of the eye. It pulled fragments straight out, minimizing the risk of further damage.

RINGING A BELL
Pressing the button of this doorbell completes a circuit in which the current passes into one terminal of the doorbell, then through the coils of the electromagnets, along the springy steel contact, into the brass screw and its mounting, and out through the other terminal. As the armature is pulled toward the electromagnets, the hammer hits the gong. At the same time, a gap opens between the contact spring and the screw, which breaks the circuit and switches off the electricity. The magnetism disappears, the spring on which the armature is mounted moves the armature back into its original position, the contacts touch and make the circuit again. The process is repeated until the button is released.

Gong

Hammer

Contact points

Contact-adjusting brass screw

Steel contact spring

Soft iron armature

Electromagnet

Spring mounting for armature

THE DOORBELL
When the current is switched on, the electromagnet attracts a nearby piece of iron. The movement of the iron, known as the armature, can be used to switch on a separate electrical circuit. In this doorbell, the armature also switches off its own circuit. Huge rows of relays are still the basis for some telephone exchanges (pp. 58–59).

(pp. 58–59)

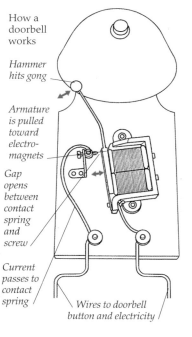

How a doorbell works

Hammer hits gong

Armature is pulled toward electro-magnets

Gap opens between contact spring and screw

Current passes to contact spring

Wires to doorbell button and electricity

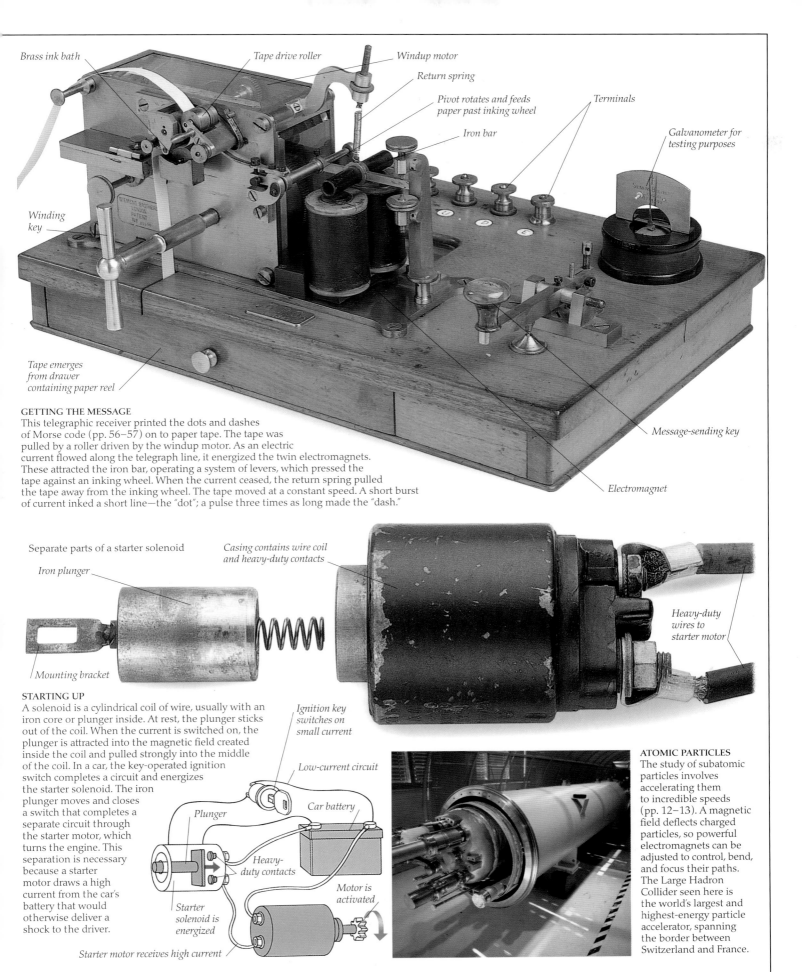

Brass ink bath

Tape drive roller

Windup motor

Return spring

Pivot rotates and feeds paper past inking wheel

Iron bar

Terminals

Galvanometer for testing purposes

Winding key

Tape emerges from drawer containing paper reel

Message-sending key

Electromagnet

GETTING THE MESSAGE

This telegraphic receiver printed the dots and dashes of Morse code (pp. 56–57) on to paper tape. The tape was pulled by a roller driven by the windup motor. As an electric current flowed along the telegraph line, it energized the twin electromagnets. These attracted the iron bar, operating a system of levers, which pressed the tape against an inking wheel. When the current ceased, the return spring pulled the tape away from the inking wheel. The tape moved at a constant speed. A short burst of current inked a short line—the "dot"; a pulse three times as long made the "dash."

Separate parts of a starter solenoid

Casing contains wire coil and heavy-duty contacts

Iron plunger

Mounting bracket

Heavy-duty wires to starter motor

STARTING UP

A solenoid is a cylindrical coil of wire, usually with an iron core or plunger inside. At rest, the plunger sticks out of the coil. When the current is switched on, the plunger is attracted into the magnetic field created inside the coil and pulled strongly into the middle of the coil. In a car, the key-operated ignition switch completes a circuit and energizes the starter solenoid. The iron plunger moves and closes a switch that completes a separate circuit through the starter motor, which turns the engine. This separation is necessary because a starter motor draws a high current from the car's battery that would otherwise deliver a shock to the driver.

Ignition key switches on small current

Low-current circuit

Plunger

Car battery

Heavy-duty contacts

Starter solenoid is energized

Motor is activated

Starter motor receives high current

ATOMIC PARTICLES

The study of subatomic particles involves accelerating them to incredible speeds (pp. 12–13). A magnetic field deflects charged particles, so powerful electromagnets can be adjusted to control, bend, and focus their paths. The Large Hadron Collider seen here is the world's largest and highest-energy particle accelerator, spanning the border between Switzerland and France.

Electricity from magnetism

FATHER OF ELECTRICITY
Michael Faraday (1791–1867) studied many areas of science, including the effects of intense magnetism on light. This phenomenon led him to ideas that were to form the foundation of electromagnetic field theory (pp. 60–61).

WHEN AN ELECTRIC GUITARIST plucks a string in a vast stadium, the metal string is almost silent. However, its vibrations are detected by an electromagnetic pickup, boosted by the amplifiers, and this fills the stadium with sound. The guitar's pickup is one of the hundreds of electrical devices, including generators and transformers, that rely on electromagnetic induction—manipulating magnetism to make electricity. The principle was demonstrated in 1831 by Michael Faraday in Britain and by Joseph Henry in the United States. In electromagnetic induction, a varying or moving magnetic field produces an electromotive force (e.m.f.) in a nearby conductor, and thus an electric current if the conductor is part of a circuit (p. 20). The current flows only while the magnetic field varies.

Magnet

Coil

First coil connected to battery

Galvanometer

Swing of pointer indicates induced current

MAGNET AND COIL
A wire can be subjected to a changing magnetic field by moving a nearby permanent magnet (above), or the changing magnetic field may come from an electromagnet (above right). In one of Faraday's experiments, a rod-shaped permanent magnet was thrust in and out of a coil of wire. The magnet was surrounded by invisible "lines of magnetic force," as might be traced out by iron filings (pp. 26–27). If the magnet is still, there is no change in the magnetic field, and no current flows. When the magnet moves, its lines of force cross the wire and so induce a current, which can be detected by a galvanometer (p. 24). The idea of "lines of magnetic force" was one of many proposed by Faraday.

Thumb shows the direction of motion

First finger points in the direction of magnetic field

Second finger points in the direction of the e.m.f.

RIGHT-HAND RULE
This useful rule helps figure out the direction of the induced current. It relates the direction of the magnetic field (north to south), the direction of movement in a generator, and the e.m.f., or current (positive to negative). The direction of movement in an electric motor is shown by the left-hand rule (p. 27).

POPULARIZING SCIENCE
This painting shows Faraday at London's Royal Institution in 1856. He gave many lectures that helped to popularize science among the general public. His rational approach to developing theories and analyzing the results is still admired.

FARADAY'S INDUCTION RING
Faraday investigated the effects of electromagnetic induction using this equipment (left). One wire is wound in a coil around part of an iron ring, with ends to connect to the terminals of a battery. A separate wire is wound around another part of the ring—it does not touch the first wire. Its ends are connected to a galvanometer. When the first coil is connected to the battery, a magnetic field builds up almost instantaneously around it, and in the iron ring. As the magnetic field forms, it induces a current in the second coil, which shows as a sudden swing of the galvanometer pointer. In a split second, the magnetic field has formed and becomes steady, so current no longer flows. If the first coil is disconnected from the battery, the magnetic field collapses, again inducing a pulse of electric current in the second coil, but in the other direction.

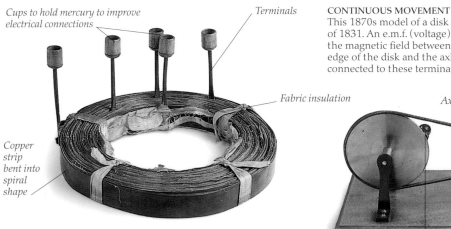

Galvanometer shows existence of current

Second coil connected to galvanometer

Soft iron ring

RECORD-KEEPING
An entry in Faraday's notebook, dated August 29, 1831, shows his sketch of the induction ring apparatus. Faraday always kept careful scientific records.

CONTINUOUS MOVEMENT
This 1870s model of a disk generator demonstrates one of Faraday's experiments of 1831. An e.m.f. (voltage) is induced in the copper disk when it is rotated in the magnetic field between the poles of the electromagnet. Spring contacts on the edge of the disk and the axle connect to terminals on the base. If a galvanometer is connected to these terminals, the circuit will be completed and a current will flow.

Cups to hold mercury to improve electrical connections

Terminals

Fabric insulation

Axle

Electromagnet creates strong magnetic field

Copper strip bent into spiral shape

HENRY'S INDUCTION COIL
Using a coil of copper strips, Joseph Henry recognized another effect known as self-inductance. He discovered that a wire carrying a changing current not only induces a voltage in nearby conductors, but also in itself. This makes it impossible to start and stop a current instantaneously. The unit of electrical inductance is called the henry.

Hand crank turns the disk

Copper disk turns in the magnetic field

Terminal

Spring contact

1889-26

Magneto-electric machines

THE RESEARCHES of Henry, Faraday, and others in the 1830s were followed gradually by practical machines that converted mechanical energy to electrical energy. These machines were known as magneto-electric machines. Later, they used electro-magnets and came to be called generators or dynamos. The earliest uses were as demonstration models and for medical treatment (pp. 50–51). Electroplating (pp. 32–33) was the earliest serious application, in 1844, followed by lighthouse illumination. It was not until the 1880s that innovations in design led to their use for electric lighting (pp. 42–43).

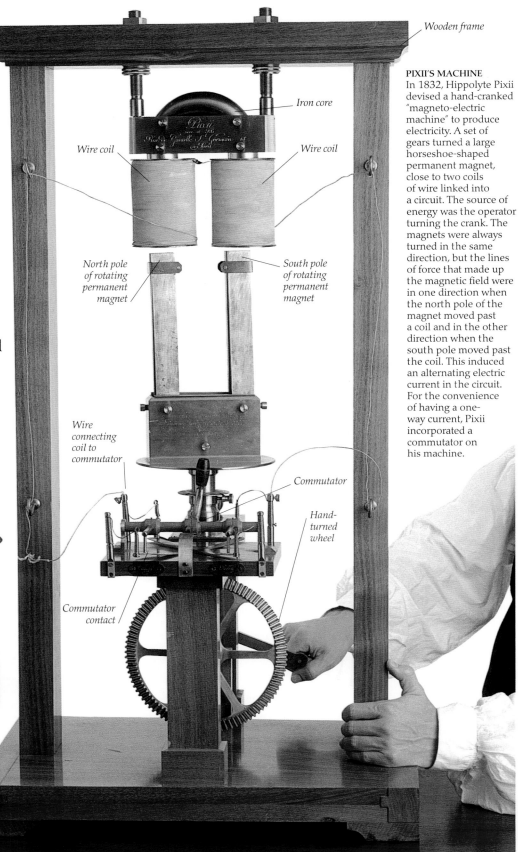

Wooden frame

Iron core

Wire coil

Wire coil

North pole of rotating permanent magnet

South pole of rotating permanent magnet

Wire connecting coil to commutator

Commutator

Hand-turned wheel

Commutator contact

PIXII'S MACHINE
In 1832, Hippolyte Pixii devised a hand-cranked "magneto-electric machine" to produce electricity. A set of gears turned a large horseshoe-shaped permanent magnet, close to two coils of wire linked into a circuit. The source of energy was the operator turning the crank. The magnets were always turned in the same direction, but the lines of force that made up the magnetic field were in one direction when the north pole of the magnet moved past a coil and in the other direction when the south pole moved past the coil. This induced an alternating electric current in the circuit. For the convenience of having a one-way current, Pixii incorporated a commutator on his machine.

CLARKE'S MACHINE
Edward Clarke, a London instrument maker, designed an efficient magneto-electric machine where turning the handle rotated coils of wire, not a large magnet, as in Pixii's machine (right). Clarke's machine was used for demonstrations and medical treatments (pp. 50–51).

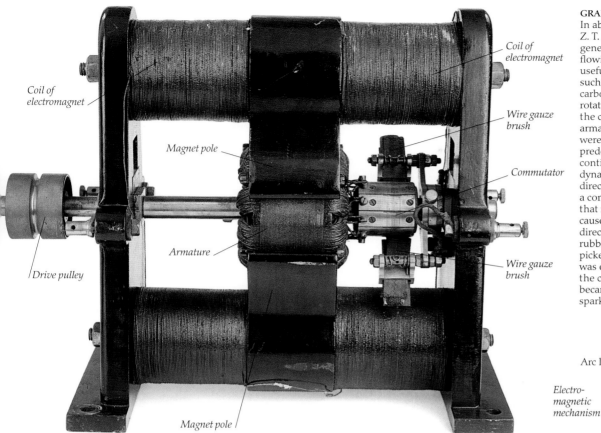

Coil of electromagnet

Coil of electromagnet

Magnet pole

Armature

Drive pulley

Wire gauze brush

Commutator

Wire gauze brush

Magnet pole

GRAMME DYNAMO

In about 1870, Belgian inventor Z. T. Gramme devised a dynamo that generated enough electric current, flowing sufficiently steadily, to be useful for large-scale applications, such as illuminating factories by carbon arc lights (below). The rotating part of the dynamo, bearing the coils of wire, is known as the armature. Gramme's dynamos were steam-driven and, unlike their predecessors, did not overheat in continuous operation. The Gramme dynamo produced a one-way or direct current (d.c.). It incorporated a commutator—segments of copper— that rotated with the armature and caused the current to flow in one direction only. Wire gauze brushes rubbing against the commutator picked up the current. The dynamo was expensive to maintain because the commutator and brush contacts became worn by pressure and the sparks that flew between them.

WERNER VON SIEMENS
The German Siemens family made many contributions to electrical engineering. Werner von Siemens (1816–92) designed a dynamo (1866) that used opposing electromagnets to produce a magnetic field around the armature, rather than around a permanent magnet (p. 36).

Carbon rods for lighting

An early use for dynamo-generated electricity was arc lighting. The arc is a "continuous spark" between carbon rods—carbon being a good conductor (p. 21). Arc lamps threw intense light, but they were inefficient, unpredictable, and needed constant attention. Even so, they were installed in lighthouses, public buildings, and street lighting.

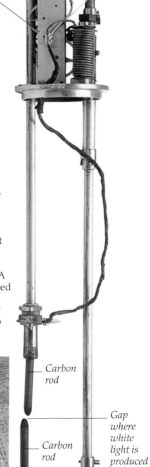

Arc lamp

Electro-magnetic mechanism

Carbon rod

Gap where white light is produced

Carbon rod

PUBLIC LIGHTING
In an arc lamp, the gap between the carbon rods is critical. It needs regular adjustment because the gap widens as the carbon vaporizes. A mechanism operated by electromagnets controls the upper carbon rod to keep the necessary gap.

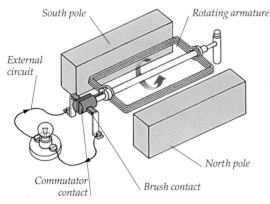

South pole

Rotating armature

External circuit

Commutator contact

Brush contact

North pole

HOW THE DYNAMO WORKS
A coil of wire (the armature) is rotated between the poles of permanent magnets. As one side of the coil travels past the north pole, it cuts the lines of magnetic force, and a current is induced. The coil moves on and the current dies away. Then it approaches the south pole, inducing a current in the opposite direction. The coil is attached to the commutator, which causes the current on the external circuit to flow in the same direction all the time.

HOW THE ARC WORKS
The electric current passes through the pointed tips of the rods as they touch. It heats them so much that the carbon vaporizes. As the rods are drawn apart, the vapor will carry the current across the small gap, glowing intensely as it does so. Davy and Faraday demonstrated arcs at their lectures (pp. 34–35).

19th-century lighthouses at La Hève, France, which used arc lamps

Making things move

In 1821, the year after Oersted's discovery of a connection between electricity and magnetism (pp. 26–27), Michael Faraday devised a simple apparatus in which a current-carrying wire rotated around a magnetic pole. It was the first electric motor, although it was too crude to have any practical use. During the 1830s, many types of primitive electric motor were built, and some were used to drive machines. The American engineer Thomas Davenport used them to turn a drill and lathe, but they were inefficient and expensive, partly because the source of electricity to drive them was a battery. By the 1870s, dynamos (p. 37) were able to provide a cheaper source of electricity, and engineers had learned that when a dynamo operated in reverse and was supplied with electric current, it made an efficient motor. The commercial use of motors grew, especially traction motors to drive trains.

Metal support arm carries current

Wire to battery

CONTINUOUS MOTION
In Faraday's "electro-magnetic rotation apparatus," electric current produced continuous movement. A stiff wire was suspended from a flexible one, so that it could move freely. The lower part of the stiff wire was placed near one pole of a permanent magnet. The end of the wire dipped into a dish of mercury (a metal that is liquid at normal room temperatures). The mercury allowed the end of the wire to move and, being a metal, it also conducted electricity. When a current flowed through the wire, this produced a magnetic field around it. The field interacted with the magnetic field around the magnet, and the wire began to move around it. The liquid mercury allowed the wire to rotate around the magnet, while still maintaining the circuit and permitting the current to flow.

BARLOW'S WHEEL
In this apparatus, devised by Peter Barlow (1776–1862) in 1823, a star-shaped metal wheel was free to rotate on an axle, within the magnetic field of a horseshoe magnet. Current flowing from a battery through the wheel set up a magnetic field around it, and so the points of the star near the horseshoe magnet moved. The points of the wheel dipped into a mercury bath below, to maintain the circuit while allowing the wheel to move.

ELECTROMAGNETIC ROTATIONS
In a drawing of one of Faraday's versions, a wire rotated around a magnet (right), while in another (left), the magnet rotated around a fixed wire.

Rotating conductor

Bar magnet

Liquid mercury

Glass dish

Wire to battery

ELECTROMAGNETIC ENGINE

This 1835 model was typical of the engines of the time in that it used reciprocating motion like pistons in the cylinder of a steam engine (p. 42). These engines were not successful because they reflected contemporary steam engine technology, which was inappropriate for electricity.

Hinged arm is drawn down

Iron bar

Wheel turns

Small arm is pulled down

Electromagnets attract iron bar

THE ELECTRIC TRAIN

In the 1870s, the Siemens company in Germany (p. 37) experimented with electric motors strong enough to pull a train. The Siemens electric railroad was demonstrated at the Berlin Trade Exhibition in 1879.

EDISON'S ELECTRIC PEN

In 1880, this early commercial application of a small electric motor relied on current from a battery. The spinning motor operated a treadle system that made the needle inside the pen jab up and down 130 times each second. The needle point was used to perforate a stencil sheet, from which multiple copies could be made with an ink roller.

HOW THE MOTOR WORKS

In a simple electric motor, current flows through a coil of wire (the armature) between the poles of a permanent magnet. When a current flows through any wire in a magnetic field, there is a force on it (p. 27). The forces on the coil push one side of it down and the other side up. The commutator (p. 37) on the end of the rotating shaft reverses the direction of the current through the coil twice every revolution, which keeps the coil rotating in the same direction.

South pole

Rotating coil of armature

Battery

North pole

Commutator

Brush contacts

1930s sewing machine

Close-up of 1930s sewing machine

Shaft

MOTORS ENTER THE HOME

When Isaac Singer produced his sewing machine in 1850, one breakthrough was the foot-operated treadle, which left both hands free. In the 1930s, another new attachment appeared—an electric motor to work the needle and bobbin housing. The motor has outer electromagnets and a multicoil inner armature (p. 40). Small, powerful electric motors opened up a new world of tools and gadgets. Compared to many other machines, the modern electric motor is extremely efficient. It turns more than 90 percent of the energy fed into it, as electricity, into the energy of motion. Today, many everyday appliances, from vacuum cleaners to refrigerators, hair dryers and electric drills, use electric motors of one kind or another.

Coils of armature

Coils of electromagnet

Iron core

Electrical socket

Crank system to drive bobbin

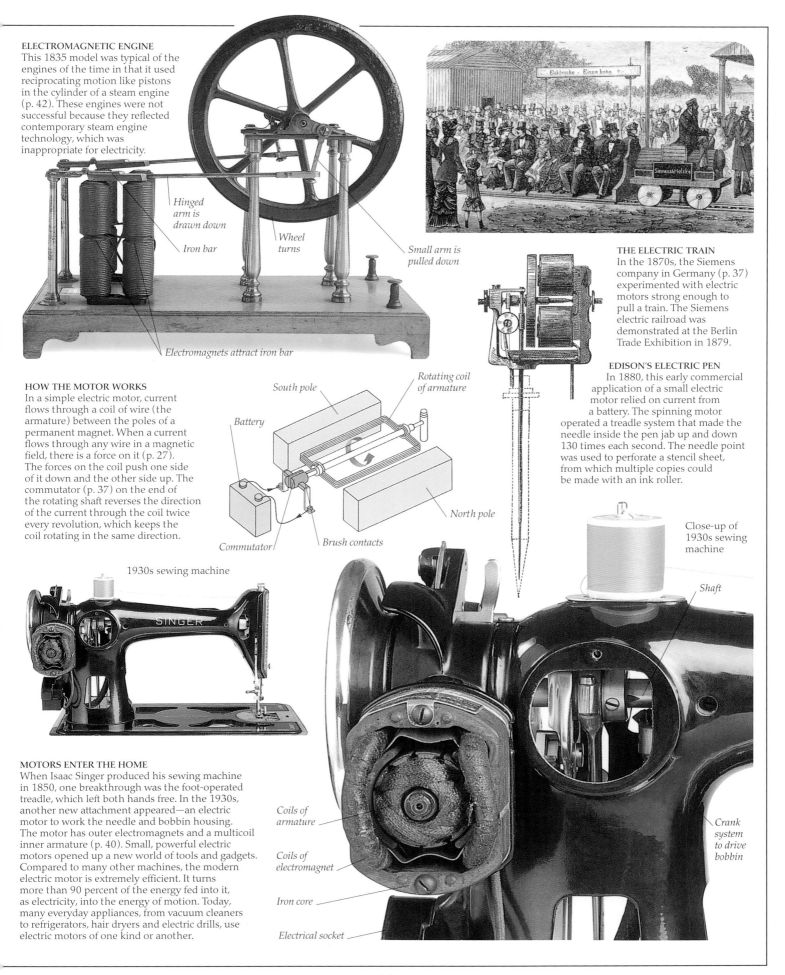

Manipulating electricity

Michael Faraday's induction ring (p. 35), with two electrically separate coils, was in effect the first transformer. A transformer can alter the voltage of an electricity supply by having a different number of turns in each coil. Sending electricity long distances through power cables is more efficient at high voltages than at low ones. Transformers boost voltage for transmission, then reduce it at the other end for everyday use. Since a transformer works by electromagnetic induction and requires a varying magnetic field, it cannot work with direct current (d.c.). It operates using alternating current (a.c.), which rises to a peak flowing one way, fades, and rises again in the reverse direction.

Terminal of coil B

Twine

Terminal of coil B

FARADAY'S RING
This soft iron ring, wound with coils of copper wire separated by twine and muslin, was used by Faraday in his discovery of electromagnetic induction (pp. 34–35). Faraday found that electric current in the coil he marked A induced an electric current in coil B, although the wires did not touch. This ring was the first transformer, although it was not used as such, because Faraday did not have alternating current. He used the direct current from a battery.

Iron ring

Terminal of coil A

Terminal of coil A

Copper wire

Muslin covering

Slip rings

Brush contact

Current flows one way

South pole

First half-turn of armature

North pole

Brush contact

A.C. GENERATOR
An alternator is a type of generator that produces a.c. Unlike a d.c. dynamo (p. 37), it lacks a commutator to reverse the connections in the circuit. Instead, brushes press continuously on slip rings. As the armature rotates, the induced current flows one way for half a turn (as a part of the coil passes the north pole), then flows the other way for the other half-turn (as it passes the south pole). Speed of rotation determines how quickly the current reverses.

Second half-turn of armature

South pole

Current flows the other way

North pole

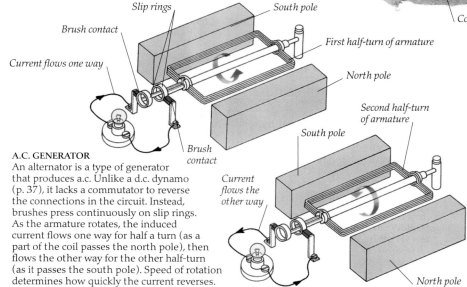

CHARLES STEINMETZ
Steinmetz (1865–1923) studied in Germany and moved to the United States in 1889, where he worked as an electrical engineer. From the 1890s, he studied the behavior of alternating current circuits and developed the theory that allowed engineers to design a.c. circuits and devices. With scientists such as Tesla (right), he helped to make a.c. a practical proposition for households.

Nikola Tesla

Tesla (1856–1943), who was born in Croatia to Serbian parents, emigrated to the United States in 1884. He worked briefly for Thomas Edison. Several years earlier, Tesla had realized how he could build an a.c. motor that would not need a commutator (p. 37). In 1888, he built his first "induction motor." This was a major factor in the widespread adoption of a.c. supplies. The induction motor is probably still the most widely used type of electric motor today. Tesla also invented a type of transformer, the Tesla coil, which works at very high frequencies and produces enormous voltages.

READING IN A THUNDERSTORM
Tesla imagined that one day even the power of lightning bolts could be harnessed. This photograph shows him reading at his high-voltage research laboratory in the United States in 1899, surrounded by giant sparks and bolts of electricity.

INDUCTION MOTOR
The induction motor has no brushes or commutators. It uses a "rotating magnetic field," made by rapidly feeding carefully timed alternating currents to a series of outer windings—the stator—to produce a magnetic field pattern that rotates. The inner set of windings on the shaft is the rotor. The stator's magnetic field induces a current in the rotor, and this becomes an electromagnet, too. As the stator's magnetic field pattern rotates, it "drags" the rotor with it.

Stator winding

Brass frame

Rotor

Wooden base

Rotor shaft

Rods form part of brass frame

Connection to a.c. electricity supply

STEPPING UP OR DOWN
The change of voltage in a transformer depends on the number of turns in the two coils, called the primary and secondary windings. If the secondary has more turns than the primary, voltage is increased (stepped up). If it has fewer, voltage is decreased (stepped down). There is no magical gain—as voltage rises, current falls, keeping the overall electrical energy the same.

Step-up transformer

Primary windings to electricity source

Secondary windings connected to high voltage lines

Step-down transformer

Primary windings to electricity source

Secondary windings connected to load—electric motors

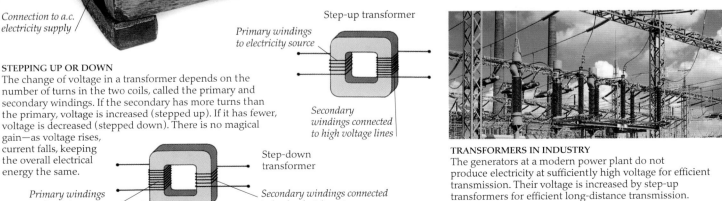

TRANSFORMERS IN INDUSTRY
The generators at a modern power plant do not produce electricity at sufficiently high voltage for efficient transmission. Their voltage is increased by step-up transformers for efficient long-distance transmission.

Early electricity supplies

THROUGHOUT THE MID 19TH CENTURY, visionaries attempted to put electricity to practical use and even replace steam power, but with no results except for electroplating (p. 33), some instances of arc lighting (p. 37), and a few small models. In the 1860s, efficient generators such as steam turbines were developed, and electricity became available on a larger scale. In the 1880s, the rocketing demand for incandescent lamps (pp. 46–47) provided the stimulus for electricity distribution networks. At first, all electricity was generated at the place where it was to be used. This remained the case for a long while until the first central generating plants (pp. 43–45) were built and took over from the small, isolated units.

STEAM ENGINES
James Watt (1736–1819) was a Scottish engineer who made important improvements to the steam engine, thereby helping to stimulate the Industrial Revolution. The unit of power, the watt, is named after him. In electricity, the number of watts is obtained by multiplying volts by amps (p. 25).

THE PARSONS STEAM TURBINE
At first, generators were driven by reciprocating engines in which the steam pressure pushed pistons to and fro in cylinders; the pistons operated cranks that turned a shaft; and a pulley on the shaft drove a loop or belt, which turned the generator shaft. Charles Parsons (1854–1931) (right) patented his design for a steam turbine in 1884 in which steam alone rotated the shaft. His steam turbine was smaller, more efficient, and produced less noise and vibration than the reciprocating design. Steam at high pressure blew over the stubby, angled turbine blades, like a high-pressure windmill. The blades were on the same shaft as the armature of the dynamo, and they made it spin rapidly. The Parsons dynamo incorporated novel features so that it would work at high speed. The first turbine generators produced about 4,000 watts of electric power at 100 volts (d.c.).

Pipe from governor to diaphragm

Diaphragm

Steam control valve

Charles Parsons

Steam inlet

Turbine blades

Main shaft

Bearing to support shaft

Strong casing (cutaway)

Bearing to support shaft

Electromagnet produces magnetic field

ELECTRICITY FROM STEAM
Inside a steam generator, steam at pressure is fed through a central inlet into the turbine section, which consists of a spinning shaft inside a strong casing. Half the steam flows in each direction. It rushes through an array of alternate moving turbine blades, which it pushes around, and fixed guide vanes, which guide it in the most efficient way. As steam progresses, its pressure drops but the Parsons turbine distributes this drop in pressure along the blades. The long shaft has a 15-coil armature and commutator mounted near one end. The magnetic field around the armature is produced by the field coils—electromagnets on a horseshoe-shaped iron core.

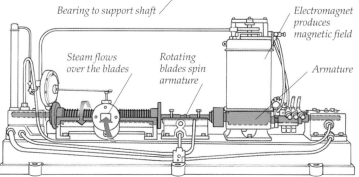

Steam flows over the blades

Rotating blades spin armature

Armature

How the steam turbine works

Electricity to the people

Thomas Edison (1847–1931) began his career as a telegrapher on North American railroads. He turned to inventing, developing things that people might want that he could patent and sell. His first moneymaker, in 1870, was an improved stock ticker. This device communicated stock and share prices telegraphically between offices in New York's financial district. There followed a string of inventions and improvements to other people's inventions. Edison was a central figure in the move toward large-scale distribution of electricity to factories, offices, and homes. One of his commercial goals was to break the monopoly of the gas companies, which he considered unfair.

Thomas Edison

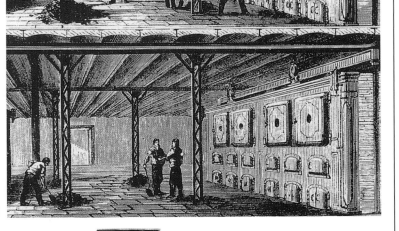

Electrical control governor regulates steam pressure via pipe to diaphragm

Field coils—electromagnets on horseshoe-shaped core

Armature

Brush contact

Commutator

Bearing to support shaft

HORSE-DRAWN POWER
The early Parsons turbine generators could be moved by means of a horse-drawn cart to the required site. Their uses were varied. Some were used to provide temporary electric lighting. In 1886, this practical Parson's turbine was used to provide the electric light for ice-skating after dark in the northeast of England when a local pond froze.

PEARL STREET PLANT
In 1882, Edison and his colleagues installed steam boilers and improved dynamos in a building on Pearl Street, New York City, shown here in this stylized engraving. He had cables installed to distribute the current to the surrounding city district south of Wall Street. Edison manufactured light-bulbs and all the other components needed to make it easy for people to equip their homes for electric lighting.

CITY LIGHTS
Before incandescent lights (p. 47), some city streets were lit by electric arc lamps, as in this New York scene of 1879. But the light was unpleasantly glaring and unreliable (p. 37), so gas was used for most street lighting.

The power plant

An ELECTRICITY SUPPLY is regarded as a major requirement for a modern "civilized" society. In the late 19th century, electricity-generating power plants were being installed in many of the world's large cities, although it was some decades before the suburbs, and then the rural areas, received service. Today, electricity is such a familiar and convenient form of energy that it is simply called "power"—a word with its own scientific meaning (the rate at which energy is used). The majority of modern power plants use turbines to turn generators. These turbines are turned by running water in hydroelectric power plants, or by steam obtained from water boiled by the heat from burning coal, oil, nuclear fuel, or some other source. Less-developed areas may obtain their electricity from local generators.

BIGGER AND BETTER
This model shows the planned Deptford Central Plant of the London Electricity Supply Corporation. The engineer who designed it, Sebastian Ferranti (1864–1930), believed it would be more economical to build large power plants outside cities where land was cheap, and to transmit the power at high voltage to subplants near the users. Unfortunately, he was ahead of his time. Bureaucracy and technical problems kept the plant from being completed. The machines on the right-hand side were installed and supplied power. The enormous ones on the left were never finished.

Flat copper coils

Feed pipes

Flywheel

Connecting rod to crank shaft

Check valve

POWER FOR NEW YORK
Great power plants, such as this Edison Company plant in New York, were often built on riverbanks or coastlines. The coal to fire the boilers could be delivered by barge, and river or seawater supplied the cooling requirements. Electricity changed people's lives, but smoke belched from the chimneys and soot settled over neighborhoods.

DISTRIBUTION NETWORK
A typical power plant generator produces alternating current at 25,000 volts. This is stepped up to hundreds of thousands of volts to reduce the energy loss during long-distance transmission. A main subplant step-down transformer (pp. 40–41) reduces the voltage for the local area. Smaller subplant transformers reduce it further for distribution to offices and homes.

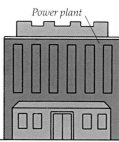
Power plant

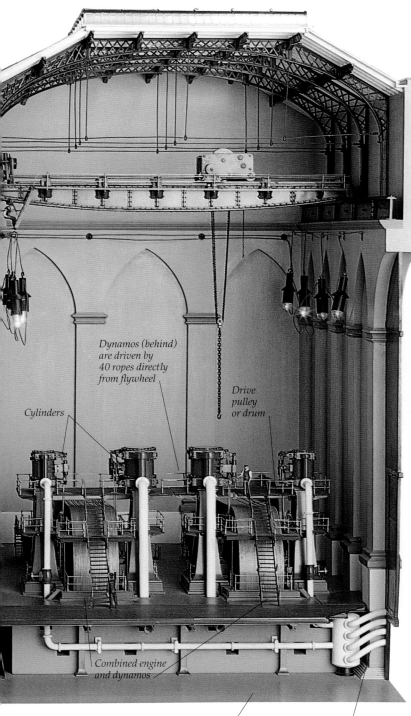

Dynamos (behind) are driven by 40 ropes directly from flywheel

Drive pulley or drum

Cylinders

Combined engine and dynamos

Thick concrete floor to support heavy machinery

Feed pipes from boiler

Renewable energy

The production of electricity is using up nonrenewable sources—coal, oil, and gas. Sustainable or renewable energy sources that will not run out are being used increasingly around the world for generation. They include rushing water in rivers as hydropower, the energy of moving air in wind turbines, and light from the Sun as solar power. Other sources are waves and tides, flammable gases from rotting plants, and heat from deep inside the Earth.

POWER FROM THE SUN
Solar panels contain many hundreds or thousands of units called photovoltaic (pv, "light-electricity") cells. Most standard cells are fingernail- to hand-sized and produce 0.5–2 volts of electricity. For best results the panels point at the noon sun. This photovoltaic power plant is located in Paris, France.

HYDROELECTRIC POWER
Glen Canyon dam on the Colorado River channels running water through great turbines that turn generators. In countries with sufficient rainfall and plentiful fast rivers, such as New Zealand, hydroelectric plants generate most of the total electricity needs.

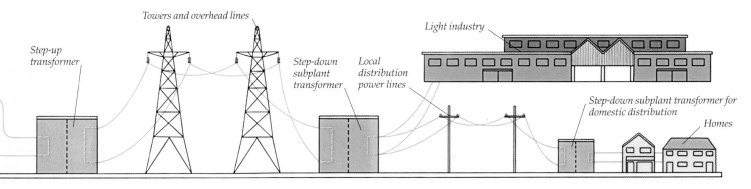

Towers and overhead lines

Step-up transformer

Step-down subplant transformer

Local distribution power lines

Light industry

Step-down subplant transformer for domestic distribution

Homes

Electricity in the home

ELECTRICITY WAS FIRST WIRED from power plants into homes, offices, and factories in the 1880s, in big cities such as New York, London, and Paris. Its first major use was for lighting—and it seemed both miraculous and mysterious. More convenient than gas lights, oil lamps, and candles, the flick of a switch could now transform night into day. In 1882, Thomas Edison's factories made 100,000 lightbulbs, but because of the years it took to lay cables and establish electricity locally, electric light was not easily available until the 1930s. The new power was dangerously invisible. A wire looked the same, whether it was carrying a current or not. Early users were warned of the new dangers, although electricity was still safer than the naked flames of candles and gas.

THE MESSAGE
By 1900, demand for electric lightbulbs in the United States was 45 million.

Early electric meter

ELECTRICITY METERS
An early meter (left), pioneered by Thomas Edison, used electrolysis (pp. 32–33) to measure the electricity consumed. The current passed through copper sulfate solution in the jars. The passage of the electric current caused the copper to dissolve on one plate and be deposited on the other. The change in weight of the plates was proportional to the electricity used. The wavy resistance wire and the lamp below prevented the solution from freezing in winter. By the 1930s, the meter (below) had a spinning plate moved by induction (pp. 34–35), geared to a series of dials. These showed the amount of electrical energy used, measured in kilowatt-hours (1,000 watts of power for one hour of time).

Jar containing copper sulfate solution

Copper plates

Resistance wire

Lamp to provide heat

1930s meter

Dials showing kilowatt hours

READING THE METER
Officials from electricity companies were soon visiting consumers on a regular basis to read the electricity meter. The meter reader switched off the supply, removed the copper plate, replaced it with a new one, and took the plate away for weighing. In this way the company determined how much the consumer should pay.

Spinning plate moved by induction

Electric lamps

Around 1880, lightbulbs were developed by Edison, Joseph Swan (1828–1914), and others. These bulbs were called filament or incandescent bulbs because of the way they worked. Electricity flowed through a thin piece of carbon with high resistance—the filament. This became so hot that it glowed white, or incandesced. If the filament glowed, oxygen in the air would combine with it and quickly burn it away. So air was sucked out of the bulb to create a vacuum around the filament.

Filament lightbulb

THE FILAMENT BULB
The filament lightbulb works on the same principle as the Edison-Swan versions, but the materials have changed. The filaments made of tungsten can now withstand very high temperatures. The filament may be 20 in (50 cm) long, but coiled tightly to take up little space. An inert gas such as argon, to reduce evaporation of the tungsten, has replaced the vacuum.

Bulb fits into ceramic safety cover

Wires carry electricity to and from filament

Filament support

Inert gas such as argon

Hard metal tungsten filament

FLUORESCENCE
The French scientist Antoine Becquerel (1852–1908) used fluorescent light in his discovery of radioactivity. This type of light works when a substance gives off light after being stimulated by other rays, such as invisible ultraviolet (UV) light. However, practical fluorescent lamps were not in use until the 1950s.

Edison screw-in bulb

Contact metal end

Metal screw fitting

Carbonized bamboo filament

Wires carrying electricity to and from filament

Vacuum within bulb

TURNING ON THE LIGHT
This early electrical switch has the metal components in a ceramic body. Two metal arms are sprung so they flick quickly from one position to another. When the switch is turned on, the arms slot into U-shaped springy contacts, so completing the electrical circuit. This must happen fast, and the contacts must be good, or the electricity will spark across any gaps and cause damage.

Switch turned on

Sprung metal arm

Circuit completed

Switch turned off

Ceramic body

Circuit broken here

Glass discharge tube

SAVING POWER
"Low-energy" bulbs or compact fluorescent lamps, CFLs, have mostly replaced filament bulbs. They use between four and eight times less electricity for the same light output, which comes from the fluorescent coating inside the tube, and last between 10 and 20 times longer.

Electrical appliances

As soon as electricity was available in houses, people began to think up new uses for it. Although the early 20th century saw the invention and design of "labor-saving" appliances to make domestic life easier, the electric iron was the only appliance commonly found in the home, along with electric lights. Most early appliances used the ability of electricity to generate heat in appliances like hair curling tongs. When electric motors (pp. 38–39) came into wide use in the 1900s, electricity could be converted into movement. The range of appliances grew to include small heaters, food mixers, and hair dryers. However, the large appliances, such as the vacuum cleaner, were still only found in more affluent homes.

ELECTRIC COOKING
Still rare, electric cooking in the 19th century offered freedom from the smoke, burning coals, and hot ashes of the traditional stove. Hotplates could be switched on and off and adjusted in temperature to give the cook greater control.

Arc jumps here

Carbon rod

Insulated wire

Wooden handle

Connection for electric flex

Heavy cast-iron base

SMOOTHING IRON
The first electric irons used a high-temperature electric spark for a heat source. This was an arc, jumping between carbon rods. The rods burned away, so they had to be manually slid together when the electricity was turned off to maintain the correct gap between them. Like the carbon arc lights, which used the same principle (p. 37), this method of changing electricity into heat was unsafe and unreliable. In 1883, the safety iron was patented in the United States. It replaced the carbon rods with a heating element.

Individual fuses   *Indicator light*

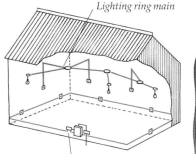

Lighting ring main

Power ring circuit

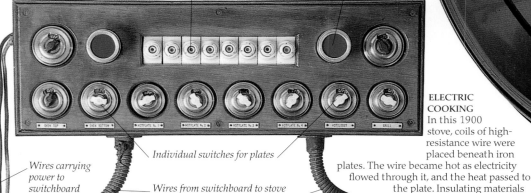

Wires carrying power to switchboard and stove

Individual switches for plates

Wires from switchboard to stove encased in corrugated metal

Iron plate

High-resistance wire inside insulated cast-iron case

HOUSEHOLD CURRENT
Most modern houses have different electrical circuits serving different needs. The basic circuits are for lighting fixtures and to carry electricity to the wall sockets. The power circuit usually has thicker cables, since it may have to supply appliances that require a high current. In some countries, there is a separate heavy-duty circuit to provide electricity to heavy appliances.

ELECTRIC COOKING
In this 1900 stove, coils of high-resistance wire were placed beneath iron plates. The wire became hot as electricity flowed through it, and the heat passed to the plate. Insulating materials were necessary to prevent electricity from flowing from the wire to the plate.

ELECTRIC KETTLE

Copper reflecting dish

Wire safety grill

Water and electricity are a dangerous combination, since water is an electrical conductor. The first electric kettles had a separate compartment for the element beneath the water. The element heated the container itself but most heat passed into the air. The Swan electric kettle of 1921 was the first with a fully insulated, waterproof heating element in the water.

Wooden handle

High-resistance coiled wire

Heating element

Copper body

Electric motor

THE ELECTRIC PERCOLATOR

One of the chief advantages of an electrical appliance is that it can be moved around and used wherever there is a socket. This 1912 coffee maker is plugged in to an electric light socket.

Hinge to raise beaters

THE MOTORIZED MIXER

Mixing, whisking, and beating ingredients by hand is a tiring and time-consuming process. This 1918 food beater and mixer was one of the earliest to be driven by a small electric motor.

Whisk

Supporting base for bowl

Current-carrying wire

ELECTRIC FIRE

The curly, high-resistance heating element in this 1930s portable heater glows a comforting red as electricity is pushed through it. The copper dish reflects the radiant heat. The types of wire used here show the principle of resistance (pp. 22–23); the high-resistance wire is used as the heating source because it glows hot while the insulated connecting wires that carry current stay cool and safe to the touch.

Electricity and medicine

THE WATERY SOLUTION OF CHEMICALS in living tissue makes a moderately good electrical conductor. Galvani noted the responses of dissected frog nerves and muscles to discharges from an electrostatic machine (p. 16), and many scientists detected electricity by the shocks it gave them. The body's own "electrical signals" are very small, measured in microvolts, and travel along nerves, sometimes at great speed. They detect, coordinate, and control, especially in the sense organs, brain, and muscles. If increasingly powerful electrical pulses are fed into the body, they cause tingling and then pain; they can send muscles into uncontrolled spasm, burn, render unconscious, and kill. However, doctors have discovered that, used carefully, electricity can diagnose, heal, and cure. Today, electrically heated scalpels slice and then seal small blood vessels to reduce bleeding during an operation. Controlled currents passing through tissue can relieve pain. Delicate surgery can be performed with electrical laser scalpels.

Horseshoe magnet

Terminal

Velvet-covered spinning coils

Tip that touches skin

A CURIOUS TREATMENT
This electro-medical machine of the 1850s had a handle and series of gear wheels that whirled coils of wire next to a horseshoe magnet, to generate electric current in the coils. A simple switch mechanism used this current and the self-inductance of the coils to produce a series of high-voltage pulses that caused an electric shock. The operator held the metal applicators by their insulating wooden handles and applied the tips to the skin of the patient (below), so the pulses traveled through the tissues to treat rheumatism, headaches, and aching joints. When it was discharged through the patient's tissues, the shock often made the muscles contract uncontrollably.

EXECUTION
Movie villains sometimes meet their end in a dazzling flash of electricity. The reality is the electric chair, and the accidental electrocutions that occur each year in factories, offices, and homes as a result of carelessness.

CONTROLLING ANIMALS
In the 19th century, electricity was sometimes used for controlling vicious horses. A generator was operated by the driver to deliver a shock via a wire in the rein and the metal bit into the horse's mouth.

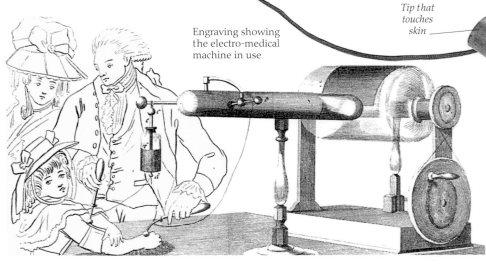

Engraving showing the electro-medical machine in use

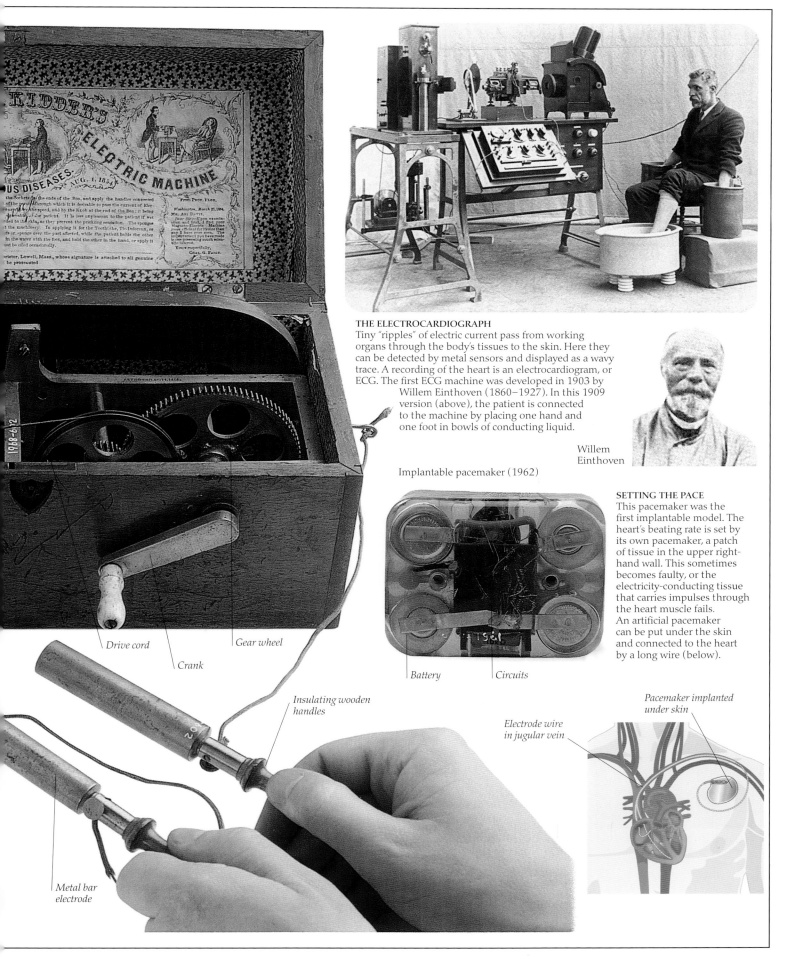

THE ELECTROCARDIOGRAPH

Tiny "ripples" of electric current pass from working organs through the body's tissues to the skin. Here they can be detected by metal sensors and displayed as a wavy trace. A recording of the heart is an electrocardiogram, or ECG. The first ECG machine was developed in 1903 by Willem Einthoven (1860–1927). In this 1909 version (above), the patient is connected to the machine by placing one hand and one foot in bowls of conducting liquid.

Willem Einthoven

Implantable pacemaker (1962)

SETTING THE PACE

This pacemaker was the first implantable model. The heart's beating rate is set by its own pacemaker, a patch of tissue in the upper right-hand wall. This sometimes becomes faulty, or the electricity-conducting tissue that carries impulses through the heart muscle fails. An artificial pacemaker can be put under the skin and connected to the heart by a long wire (below).

Drive cord

Crank

Gear wheel

Battery

Circuits

Insulating wooden handles

Metal bar electrode

Pacemaker implanted under skin

Electrode wire in jugular vein

Heat, pressure, and light

Electricity can be produced directly from heat, pressure, and light. When heat is applied to one of the junctions of two conductors so that the two junctions are at different temperatures, an electrical potential is generated; this is thermoelectricity. In the piezoelectric effect, an electrical potential is generated between opposite faces of crystals made from substances such as quartz, when the crystals are compressed—in simple terms, when the crystal is squeezed or stretched. In the photoelectric effect, light rays cause certain substances to give up electrons (p. 20) and produce an electric charge or current. In the photovoltaic effect, light produces an electrical potential between layers of different substances, so current flows in a circuit without the need for an electricity source.

THOMAS SEEBECK
In the 1820s, German scientist Thomas Seebeck (1770–1831) studied the effects of heat on conductors. This "Seebeck effect" is now known as thermoelectricity. There have been many attempts at using thermoelectricity. Its main use today is for thermometers (below right).

THE SEEBECK EFFECT
In a circuit of two metal strips joined at their ends, Seebeck heated the junction at one end and saw a compass needle between the strips swing. Seebeck thought the heat was creating magnetism. In fact, an electric current was generated when the junctions were at different temperatures, and the magnetic field this produced deflected the compass needle. The Seebeck effect is effective only with certain conductors. Seebeck obtained his best results with the dissimilar conductors bismuth and antimony. A similar effect can be produced using iron and copper. The "opposite" is the Peltier effect, named after French scientist Jean Peltier (1785–1845). A temperature difference is produced between the junctions when an electric current from a battery flows around the circuit.

Reconstruction of Seebeck's experiment

Copper strip

Current flows around circuit

Junction at room temperature

Deflected compass needle

Junction being heated

Metal base

Iron strip

Bunsen burner

MAKING A THERMOCOUPLE
One application of the Seebeck effect is the type of thermometer based on a thermocouple (opposite). Above, the probe of the thermocouple is being made by welding a wire of platinum to a wire of platinum-rhodium alloy.

PIEZOELECTRIC EFFECT

In the crystal pickup of a record player, mechanical vibrations produced in the stylus by the grooves in the record are transmitted to the piezoelectric crystal by a plastic stirrup. This produces a varying electrical signal to match the intended sound. The vibrations are directed in two directions, at right angles, to make the two channels necessary for stereophonic sound. The signal is amplified and then fed to loudspeakers (p. 61). Other applications of piezoelectricity include the audio bleeper and hand-squeezed spark-makers used for gas oven and burner lighters.

Quartz crystals inside case

To amplifier for left channel

To amplifier for right channel

Crystals produce voltage for amplification

Quartz crystals

Vibrations in stirrup transfer to quartz

Groove in vinyl record

Vibrations in stylus transfer to stirrup

LP·S ST 17D

Plastic stirrup

Stylus

PIERRE CURIE

The piezoelectric effect was first studied in about 1880 by Pierre Curie (1859–1906) and his brother Paul-Jacques (1856–1941). It is named from the Greek word *piezein*, meaning to press. The Curies used Rochelle salt and quartz, natural crystals with piezoelectric qualities. Today, synthetic crystals are used.

Intensity of light produces voltage

Transparent gold layer

Connection to meter measuring current

PHOTOVOLTAIC CELL

This cell can be connected to a galvanometer (p. 24); the flowing current indicates the intensity of the light on the cell. This is the basis for one type of photographic exposure meter. The reading helps the photographer to determine the setting for the camera.

Connecting wire

digitherm

°C

Digital reading

Probe handle

THERMOCOUPLE THERMOMETER

This device is based on the Seebeck effect. One junction of the thermocouple is at the tip of the probe. The thermocouple produces a voltage that depends on the difference between the temperature of this junction and the room temperature. The electronic circuitry in the display unit converts the voltage to a temperature difference, compensates for room temperature, and displays the result as a digital reading. This thermometer uses a nickel-chromium and nickel-aluminum thermocouple and measures temperatures from −58° F to 1830° F (−50° C to 999° C). Other types have a wider range. These thermometers have replaced the mercury type for many uses.

Probe tip

PHOTOELECTRICITY IN SPACE

Like most spacecraft the Earth-orbiting Hubble Space Telescope, launched in 1990, needs electricity to operate. This comes from large winglike solar panels or arrays that can swivel to point directly at the Sun. Hubble's panels have been replaced twice by Space Shuttle servicing missions, in 1993 and 2002. The newest panels produce 2,800 watts of electricity.

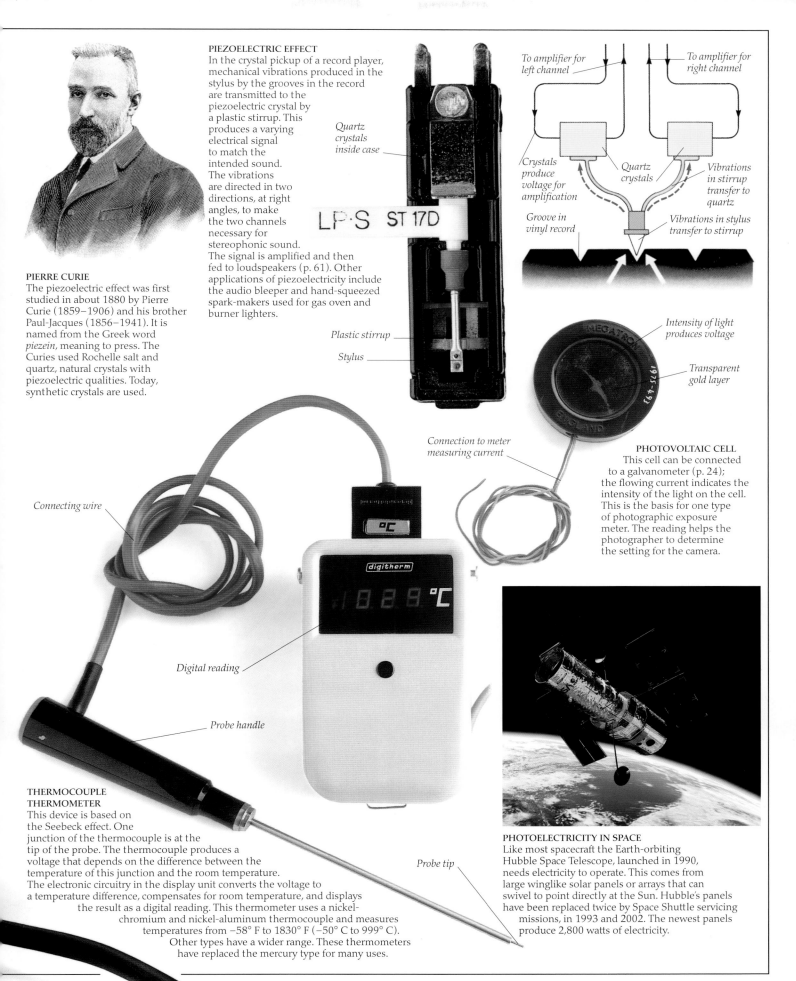

Investigating cathode rays

I⊤ WAS KNOWN IN THE 18TH CENTURY that a gas at low pressure inside a tube could be made to glow by passing a discharge from an electrostatic machine through it. In the latter part of the 19th century, new electrical apparatus enabled scientists to study the effect more thoroughly. For instance, improved vacuum pumps allowed the air pressure inside the tubes to be reduced. At very low pressures the glow disappeared and was replaced by invisible rays that came from the cathode or negative terminal and made the glass of the tube containing the gas glow green where the rays struck it. In 1883, Edison noticed that particles seemed to be given off from the negative ends of the filaments of his electric lightbulbs. The British scientist William Crookes was one of the discoverers of these "cathode rays." Later, J. J. Thomson extended this work with insights that led to the new science of atomic physics and to the discovery of the structure of the atom by Ernest Rutherford (1871–1937) and his team. The cathode ray tube became the basis for the television set (pp. 62–63) and radar equipment.

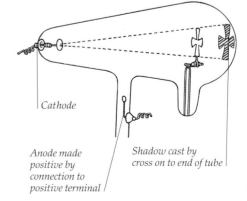

Replica of Crookes' tube

Cathode

Connection to low voltage

Tin Maltese cross

Anode

Shadow cast by cross

Connection to high voltage

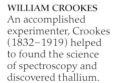

WILLIAM CROOKES
An accomplished experimenter, Crookes (1832–1919) helped to found the science of spectroscopy and discovered thallium.

CROOKES' EXPERIMENT
In the original apparatus (above) the electrons that formed the cathode rays were produced by a complex interaction between the cathode and the residual gas in the tube. In Crookes' famous experiment in 1887, a small metal cross shape was put in the path of the rays coming from the cathode. The cross cast a shadow on the glass screen beyond. This demonstrated that rays came from the cathode, and that they traveled in straight lines—just as a flashlight shining light rays on to the cross shape would cast a shadow behind it.

Crookes' Maltese cross experiment

Cathode

Anode made positive by connection to positive terminal

Shadow cast by cross on to end of tube

Front view of
modern apparatus

Thomson's tube

*Calibrations to
show deflection*

Vacuum tube

Anodes

Cathode

*Metal plates
deflect electrons
electrostatically*

*Electromagnetic coils
deflect moving electrons*

THE DISCOVERY OF THE ELECTRON

Joseph John Thomson (1856–1940) is credited with identifying the first subatomic particle, now called the electron, in 1897. Thomson knew that cathode rays could be "bent" or deflected by a magnetic field. He devised an experiment to measure the ratio of the charge carried by particles, which he believed made up cathode rays, to their mass. This involved balancing two separate forces on the particles, one produced by the magnetic field of the current flowing in a pair of coils, and the other by the electric field between two metal plates. Thomson explained his results by suggesting that cathode rays consisted of particles which carried an electric charge. This charge was equal to the charge carried by the hydrogen ions involved in electrolysis (p. 33). This proved that there was a particle even smaller than the hydrogen atom. He called it the electron.

J. J. Thomson

Fleming's tube

FLEMING'S TUBE

The Fleming tube, also called the thermionic valve or a vacuum tube, was invented by John Fleming (1849–1945) and patented in 1904. It was designed to detect the faint signals transmitted by Marconi's recently invented radio sets (pp. 60–61). A triode developed by Lee De Forest in 1906 (p. 61) was able to amplify radio signals. The cathode (negative electrode) was a hot wire that gave off electrons. These were attracted across the vacuum in the tube to the anode (positive electrode), but could not go the other way. Connected to an alternating voltage, the device thus allowed current to pass in one direction as a series of pulses. Through this capacity to amplify feeble electrical signals, the vacuum tube became the key to the development of all electronic machines.

Vacuum tube

Anode

*Hot
filament
acts as
cathode*

Supporting frame

Heated wire

MODERN DEMONSTRATION

In modern apparatuses electrons are produced more easily in larger quantity from a heated wire—the effect noticed by Edison and now called thermionic emission. The anode is given a high positive voltage. This attracts the electrons from the cathode and accelerates them. The electrons strike a fluorescent layer on the inside of the glass causing it to glow brightly—much more brightly than the plain glass of the original tubes.

Low-voltage supply

High-voltage supply

*Terminal for
electricity supply*

Communicating with electricity

TELEGRAPHY—WRITING AT A DISTANCE—was an early and successful use of electricity, coinciding with the spread of railroad networks in Europe and North America. Telegraph wires or lines were laid alongside the railroad tracks, where they were easy to check and maintain. The discoveries about the connection between electricity and magnetism (pp. 26–27) had led several people to develop the idea of sending pulses of current in coded form from one place to another. A simple on-off switch completed the circuit and allowed current to flow from the sender. This was read in a code of dots and dashes. Although it took several years for the electric telegraph to be accepted, the era of fast communication had begun.

THE WHEATSTONE TELEGRAPH
English experimenters William Cooke (1806–79) and Charles Wheatstone (1802–75) demonstrated a telegraph in England in 1837. At first, people were suspicious of the electric wires passing over their land. Wheatstone used the deflections of a needle to spell out letters, in a code of swings to the left and right. The needle was moved by the magnetic field produced by the current through coils of wire inside the case. Twisting the handle one way connected the positive terminal of the battery into the circuit and the negative one to ground, sending a current in one direction, making the needle of the receiving instrument deflect one way. Turning the handle the other way connected the negative terminal of the battery, making the needle deflect the other way.

Single-needle instrument with back removed (1846)

Coils of wire

Operating handle

Magnetic needle that acts as pointer

THE TRAIN IS COMING
Along a copper wire, the signal travels at nearly the speed of light, making telegraphy an almost instant method of sending messages. It was used extensively for signaling on the railroads. This operator listens to the clicking code through earphones; the batteries are on the floor under his desk.

Wires to telegraph

Trough battery   *Wire to battery*

A.−	J.−−−	S...	2..−−−
B−...	K.−−	T.−	3...−−
C−.−.	L.−..	U..−	4....−
D−..	M−−	V...−	5.....
E.	N−.	W.−−	6−....
F..−.	O−−−	X−..−	7−−...
G−−.	P.−−.	Y−.−−	8−−−..
H....	Q−−.−	Z−−..	9−−−−.
I..	R.−.	1.−−−−	0−−−−−

Modern Morse code alphabet

The "father of the telegraph"

American Samuel Morse (1791–1872) began his career as a professional portrait painter. The idea for a telegraph came to him in 1832, when he saw an electromagnet on a ship returning from a European tour. He gave up painting and began to investigate electromagnetism. By 1837, he had devised electromagnetic transmitters and receivers, and the first version of the code of dots and dashes that took his name and eventually became used worldwide. Morse's first permanent telegraph line, spanning 37 miles (60 km) between Baltimore and Washington, opened on May 24, 1844, with Morse's message, "What hath God wrought!"

Samuel Morse

DOTS AND DASHES

Morse's early designs for a receiver used an electromagnet and a stylus that pressed a groove into a moving paper strip. Later, there was an inking device (p. 31) for writing dots and dashes. Trained telegraphers listened to the receiver's clicks on a sounding device, decoded the message from these, and wrote it down.

Morse tapes received on the Great Eastern when it was laying the 1865 Atlantic cable

Battery

Relay

Transformer

Electromagnets

Coherer

WIRELESS RECEIVER

The wireless telegraph was an advance on telegraphy, based on electromagnetic waves. This was made possible by the early experiments of Heinrich Hertz (pp. 60–61) and the practical efforts of Guglielmo Marconi (p. 61). This wireless receiver was the same as the telegraphy receivers in that it used Morse code, but instead of a connection to a land line it had a radio receiver, which used a coherer. The coherer contains filings that increase in conductivity when they are subjected to radio waves. The link between the radio signal and the sounder circuit is made by the relay, which uses electromagnets (pp. 30–31). It passes the on-off pattern of the received current to a new, more powerful circuit.

Wire to battery

LONG-DISTANCE BUSINESS

Telegraph lines spread across the land. Their real importance was appreciated by businesses where investments and information could be received quickly. These wealthy businessmen no doubt await the 19th-century version of the latest stock market figures.

Talking with electricity

Sound waves do not travel very far in air, or very fast. As the telegraph system became established for sending messages in coded form, several inventors pursued the idea of using the complex pattern of sound waves from the voice to produce a corresponding pattern of electrical signals. These could be sent along a wire much farther and faster than sound waves in the air. At the other end, the electrical signals would be converted back to sound, to re-create the original speech. A receiver and transmitter at each end allowed both callers to speak and listen. Bell, Edison, and others succeeded in making such devices, which became known as telephones. Telegraphs retained their role of sending relatively simple messages.

ALEXANDER GRAHAM BELL
Born in Scotland, Alexander Graham Bell (1847–1922) emigrated to North America in 1870, where he became an outstanding figure in the education of the deaf. He found that different voice tones could vary the electrical signals flowing in a wire, by the process of electro-magnetic induction. He also realized that a varying signal could vibrate a flat sheet or diaphragm and produce sound waves. The principle of the telephone was born.

Bell's first telephone

THE FIRST CALL
With advice from Joseph Henry (p. 35), Bell and his assistant Thomas Watson constructed early versions of the telephone. Sound waves from the speaker's voice funneled into a chamber, where they vibrated a flat sheet of thin iron, the diaphragm. This disturbed the magnetic field of a permanent magnet, around which was wrapped a current-carrying coil connected to an external battery. The magnetic field induced varying electrical signals in the circuit, which was completed through a connection to the ground.

OPERATOR SERVICE
Only a few years after the first telephones were demonstrated, exchanges were being set up in major cities. The caller's plug had to be inserted into the correct socket. This is Croydon Exchange, near London, which opened in 1884.

Terminals

INSIDE A BELL TELEPHONE
The "candlestick" design (1878) came about due to the mistaken belief that a longer permanent magnet would be stronger than a short one. The same design (below) could function as a mouthpiece (the sound detector or microphone) or earpiece (the sound producer). Sound waves vibrate an iron diaphragm varying the magnetic field of the bar magnet, which produces varying currents in the coil by electromagnetic induction. The principle of the earpiece design changed little from Bell's time until the 1970s, though improved materials allowed the permanent magnet inside the earpiece to be smaller. It is Edison's carbon microphone that is still used for the typical mouthpiece.

The two-part telephone in use

Signal-carrying wire

Permanent bar magnet

Wooden casing

Coil of wire

Diaphragm

Funnel for sound waves

RECEIVER PRINCIPLE
In an earpiece, changing signals flow through the coils and set up a varying electromagnetic field, which interacts with the bar magnet's steady field. The overall fluctuating magnetic field attracts the iron diaphragm by varying amounts, thus vibrating it.

Signals from transmitter

Magnetic coil

Iron diaphragm

Sound waves

CARBON MICROPHONE
In a mouthpiece, a "button" of loosely packed carbon granules is connected into a circuit with a battery. Sound waves compress and expand the carbon granules, so decreasing and increasing its resistance, which varies the electrical current.

Sound waves

Battery

Signals to receiver

Iron diaphragm

Carbon granules

Cutaway of 1920s telephone handset

Permanent magnet

Signal-carrying wire

Carbon-granule button

Wire coils

Cotton pads

Diaphragm

Diaphragm

Gap

INSIDE AN EARPIECE
In this earpiece, twin wire coils act as electromagnets to vary the magnetic field of the permanent magnet. The gap between the diaphragm and magnet is critical. It should allow the diaphragm to vibrate sufficiently so the sound waves can be heard, but not let the diaphragm touch the magnet.

INSIDE A MOUTHPIECE
In the mouthpiece, the perforated screen protects the thin diaphragm underneath while still allowing sound waves to pass through. The carbon-granule "button" is surrounded by cotton pads that allow the diaphragm to vibrate freely while keeping the grains of carbon in place.

Perforated screen

Earpiece

Reed

Brass cylinder containing carbon granules

Small pair of coils

Electromagnet

Crank handle for generator to produce current to ring bell

MAKING A CALL
This telephone from 1895 contains a small hand-operated generator. When callers wished to alert the exchange, they turned the handle and generated a small electric current, which produced a signal for the operator by ringing a bell. A battery situated nearby provided current for the microphone. From about 1905, exchanges became equipped with batteries and ringing equipment, so the hand-generator design faded out.

Mouthpiece

Shaft

Magnet

THE BROWN REPEATER
From the 1900s, electromechanical repeaters were devised to copy the pattern of telephone signals into another circuit to make it stronger. In the Brown repeater, the incoming signals flowed through two small coils, producing varying magnetic fields. These vibrated a flexible metal strip called a reed. The reed was linked to a small brass cylinder containing carbon granules, which altered the current in the new circuit.

Magnet

Bell

Connecting block with terminals for battery and line

Communicating without wires

James Clerk Maxwell (1831–79) developed the findings of Faraday and other scientists, using concepts such as magnetic lines of force, and reduced the phenomena of electricity and magnetism to a group of four mathematical equations. One prediction from these equations was that an oscillating electric charge would send out "waves" of electromagnetic energy from its source. A series of experiments by Heinrich Hertz (1857–94) in the 1880s demonstrated that these waves existed, and that they could be detected at a distance. Further work by Guglielmo Marconi (1874–1937) in the 1890s resulted in wireless telegraphy, the sending of messages without wires.

JAMES CLERK MAXWELL
Scottish-born Maxwell predicted the existence of radio waves before they were demonstrated by Hertz (below). He showed that an oscillating electric charge would produce a varying electromagnetic field, which would transmit at a speed that turned out to be equal to the speed of light. From this, he suggested that light rays were electro-magnetic waves.

HERTZ'S EXPERIMENTS
Hertz demonstrated the existence of radio waves in the late 1880s. He used a device called an induction coil to produce a high voltage. One of his early transmitters consisted of two tiny coils with a spark gap. The rapidly oscillating current in the sparks between the ends of the coils produced radio waves. To detect the waves Hertz used a receiver consisting of two rods with a spark gap as the receiving antenna. A spark jumped the gap where the waves were picked up. Hertz showed that these signals had all the properties of electromagnetic waves. They could be focused by curved reflectors, and a grid of parallel wires placed in their path showed they were polarized.

Heinrich Hertz

Transmitter

Receiver

Spark appeared between coils

Induction coil produced high voltage

Polarizing screen

Radio waves

Plane reflector

Reflector

Replica of Hertz's equipment

Two coils and spark gap

Polarizing screen

GUGLIELMO MARCONI

Marconi began radio experiments on his family's estate near Bologna, Italy. He devised arrangements of long wires and metal plates to emit and receive the waves. These were the first antennas. His first radio message across the Atlantic, from Cornwall in England to Newfoundland in Canada on December 12, 1901, was Morse code for the letter "S." It established the viability of radio for long-distance communication. Here, Marconi (left) shows some of his equipment to visitors in 1920.

ELECTRICITY INTO SOUND ENERGY

Headphones were used to listen to the first radio sets. Loudspeakers were then developed so that several people could listen at once. Loudspeakers needed radios with better detectors and amplifiers. This became possible when the triode valve was devised in 1906 by Lee De Forest (1873–1961), since the valve could amplify weak signals. The loudspeaker has a strong permanent magnet shaped like a cylinder. A coil of wire fits between the poles of the magnet within the strong magnetic field and is attached to the cardboard cone. The varying electric currents pass through the coil making it move to and fro. As the coil moves, the cone moves, making sound waves that correspond to the varying electric currents.

Permanent magnet and coil in casing

Cone made from cardboard

How a loudspeaker works

Loudspeaker

Cylindrical magnet produces strong magnetic field

Varying currents passing through coil of wire vibrate cone, causing sound waves

RADIO RECEIVER

This state-of-the-art radio dates from 1925 and shows that large multi-wound antennas were required to gather the energy represented by radio waves. Each stage of circuitry in the receiver had to be individually tuned to the radio station.

The antenna frame can be rotated to produce the strongest signals

Antenna

Receiver in curved reflector

Rods pick up radio waves

Volume control

Tuning knob

Headphone socket

Touch-sensitive screen responds to tiny pulses of electricity

MODERN WIRELESS

Devices such as cell phones, tablets, laptops, desk computers, media players such as iPods, and other gadgets use various forms of "wireless" or "wi-fi" technology—that is, radio waves. Cell phones communicate with nearby masts to carry voice calls, Internet, and other information. Wireless printers, headphones, games controllers, and similar devices often use a much shorter-range radio system known as Bluetooth.

Television

IN THE AREA OF COMMUNICATION, there was another great goal for researchers and inventors. This was the wireless transmission not only of sounds, but of images, too—television. Several systems were tried for turning patterns of light into electrical signals in the camera, transmitting and receiving the signals as radio waves and displaying the received signals as a moving image for the viewer. A version of the vacuum tube, the cathode ray tube (CRT), became established as the image-displaying unit. This device was yet another stage in the two centuries of research, manipulation, and utilization of electricity—a form of energy that has become master and servant, indispensable and central to modern scientific thought.

INSIDE A 1930s TV SET
Many of the major electrical components described in this book, or their descendants, are contained in this electrical machine. The transformer and associated components produce high voltages, which drive electrons in beams from the cathode through the anodes and toward the screen (pp. 54–55). The screen has a special coating so that it fluoresces white when the electrons hit it. Variable capacitors (p. 13) and other items tune the set to receive signals from different transmitters.

Deflection coils

Screen

Cathode ray tube

Control knobs

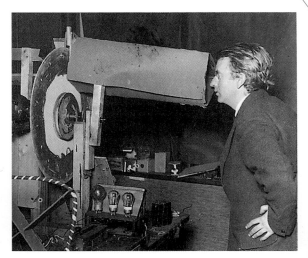

BAIRD'S MECHANICAL SCANNER
The television transmission equipment devised in the 1920s by John Logie Baird (1888–1946) was built using various pieces of scrap metal and electrical components. Central was the Nipkow disk, a fast-spinning disk with holes arranged in a spiral. As the disk turned, each hole traced a curved line and exposed part of the scene behind. A photoelectric cell (p. 53) transformed the light intensity of each part of the line into electrical signals and sent them to the receiver. Baird's 1926 version produced a 30-line image that was renewed 10 times each second. This electromechanical system was replaced by a purely electrical one (opposite).

Loudspeaker

Capacitor

HOW THE CRT TELEVISION WORKED

In the black-and-white television, electrons are produced at the cathode and are accelerated toward the positive electrode, the anode. They pass through holes in the anode and are focused by the magnetic field produced by focusing coils to produce a spot on the screen. These pairs of focusing coils, one pair arranged vertically and the other horizontally, create fields that deflect the electron beam. The fields are varied so the beam sweeps across the screen, jumps back, sweeps an adjacent line, and so on to cover the screen. At the same time, the intensity of the beam is varied by a signal applied to another electrode near the cathode. When the beam is stronger, it makes the screen glow more brightly at the spot it hits. Each second, 25 complete pictures or frames are produced. The human eye cannot follow the rapid movement of the electron beam and perceives a smoothly changing picture.

Electron beam

Four coils

Cathode

Anode

Scanned horizontal lines

Vacuum tube

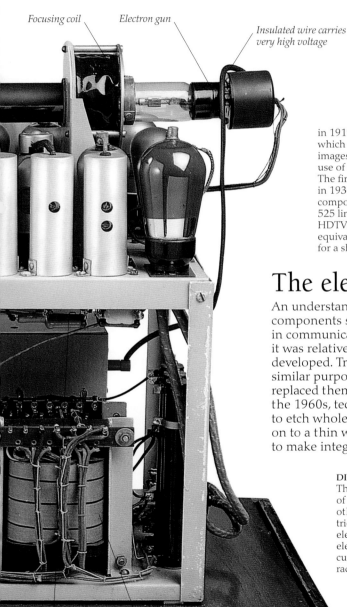

Focusing coil

Electron gun

Insulated wire carries very high voltage

Resistor

Transformer

ZWORYKIN'S CONTRIBUTIONS

Many scientists contributed to the cathode ray tube television system. Vladimir Zworykin (1889–1982) was born in Russia and moved to the US in 1919. In the 1920s, he devised the iconoscope, which used the scanning principle to convert visual images into electrical signals, and he developed the use of cathode ray tubes for displaying the images. The first regular television broadcasts began in 1936 in London, with each picture frame composed of 405 horizontal lines. Later, 525 lines were standard. Flat-screen HDTVs (High Definition) have the equivalent of more than 1,000 lines, for a sharper, clearer picture.

The electronic age

An understanding of the behavior and nature of electrons led to electronic components such as the valve (p. 55). This was an enormous breakthrough in communications but it relied on heat, wasting a great deal of energy, and it was relatively fragile. During the late 1940s, the first transistors were developed. Transistors were used for similar purposes as valves and soon replaced them for many applications. In the 1960s, techniques were introduced to etch whole networks of components on to a thin wafer or "chip" of silicon, to make integrated circuits.

DIODE VALVE

The experimental Fleming diodes of 1904 were the forerunners of other types of vacuum tube, the triode and pentode, with more electrodes. Valves could use small electrical signals and control the current and could thus amplify radio signals (pp. 60–61).

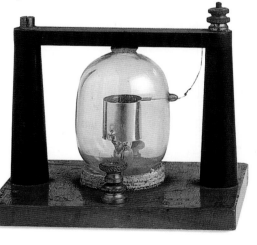

TRANSISTOR

Like valves, transistors could amplify electrical signals and manipulate currents and voltages in various ways. But they were smaller, more efficient, more robust, and eventually cheaper than valves.

SILICON CHIP

A tiny wafer of silicon has circuits containing hundreds of transistors and other electrical components.

Wafer of silicon

Did you know?

AMAZING FACTS

The electric eel is an unusual fish capable of generating powerful electrical shocks. Its shocks can keep predators away or stun an animal the eel is hunting for its own dinner. An adult can produce a shock of up to 500 volts; a juvenile gives a 100-volt strike.

Benjamin Franklin, credited with the invention of the lightning rod, worked for years to come up with the best design to "pull" lightning from the sky and direct it away from buildings. Some historians believe he began his famous kite-flying experiments because he was tired of waiting for Christ Church in Philadelphia to be finished—he had planned to try out his lightning rod on the roof of the church.

Were batteries invented in Baghdad? In 1938, the director of the National Museum of Iraq wrote a paper speculating that an object dated to about 250 BCE was used to electroplate gold and silver coatings on certain objects. This object, known as the Baghdad Battery, resembles an electrochemical cell, although there is no firm evidence to show how it was used.

"Lady Liberty" was a gift from France to the United States

Statue of Liberty

The International Space Station needs electricity to power its computers, light its interior, recycle water, and support life. But there is nowhere to plug it in! It gets its electricity from eight solar arrays, which extend from the station like huge wings. There are more than a quarter million solar cells in total on the arrays, used to capture solar power. When the ISS is orbiting in the Earth's shadow, it relies on rechargeable batteries.

Electricity travels almost at the speed of light—that's more than 186,000 miles (299,000 km) per second. If you could move that quickly, you could zip around the world nearly eight times in the same time it takes to flick on a light switch.

Introduced in 1946, the giant ENIAC (Electrical Numerical Integrator And Computer), one of the world's first computers, gobbled up 160 kilowatts of electrical power, weighed 33 tons (30 metric tons), and covered 1,800 sq ft (167 sq m). On its 50th anniversary, students at the University of Pennsylvania re-created the whole system on a microchip.

The first lighthouse in the United States to feature an electric light is also one of the most recognizable: the Statue of Liberty, in New York Harbor. The statue (officially decommissioned as a lighthouse in 1902) had a beam of light that was visible for 24 miles (39 km). Lady Liberty marks the entrance to the inner harbor of New York and the Hudson River.

When Thomas Edison's Pearl Street Station opened in New York in 1882, the plant's lone generator produced enough electricity for 800 lightbulbs. Today, the utility industry produces over 2.5 gigawatt-hours annually. That's enough to keep 4.8 billion 60-watt bulbs lit up for an entire year.

US President Benjamin Harrison held office when the White House was first wired for electricity. He was said to be afraid of getting shocked when touching the switches, so he and his wife used the original gaslights.

ENIAC, with operator

The production of electricity from biomass (including animal wastes) is helping to meet increasing global energy needs. The waste produced by one chicken in a lifetime can supply enough energy to run a low-energy lightbulb for 50 hours.

Chicken

Ever wonder how birds can sit on power lines without getting an electric shock? Electricity always tries to make its way to the ground. If something is in the way (including you) it could travel through that thing to get there. But, normally, no part of a power line is "grounded" (touching the ground), so it is safe for birds to sit there.

Birds on a wire

As late as 1993, high-tech electrical gadgets such as personal computers, printers, and video games had a negligible effect on the average American family's power usage. Today, however, these items are estimated to account for more than 13 percent of a typical household energy budget, a figure that is expected to double by the year 2020.

Q What are the most common sources of electricity in the world today?

A Recent figures show coal is still the most common source, providing up to 40 percent of electrical power. Natural gas contributes 20 percent, hydropower 18 percent, nuclear 11 percent, oil 5 percent, and renewables 6 percent.

Q What are the nonrenewable sources used to make electricity?

A Coal and natural gas are considered fossil fuels because they formed from the buried remains of plants and animals that lived millions of years ago. Uranium ore is not a fossil fuel, but it is mined and converted to a fuel used in nuclear power plants to make electricity. These energy sources are nonrenewable because they cannot be replenished in a short period of time.

Q What are the renewable sources used to make electricity?

A Sources that can be replenished easily are called renewable energy sources. The five used most often around the world today are moving water, sunlight, wind, geothermal energy, and biomass.

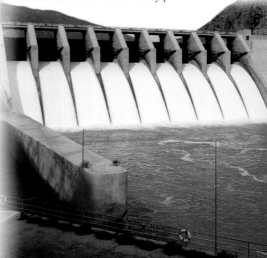

Giant turbines at a wind farm in California

Q What is hydropower? What are its advantages and disadvantages?

A Hydropower (energy derived from moving water) accounts for 7 percent of US power generation and 45 percent of renewable generation. It is considered by many the ideal fuel. It is free (aside from the cost of building the power plant), there are no waste products, and there is no pollution. But it can affect natural habitats and can only be produced where there are ample amounts of moving water.

Q What is solar power and what are its strengths and drawbacks?

A Sunlight can be converted directly or indirectly into other forms of energy. The term "solar power" usually refers to power created by solar panels, which use photovoltaic cells to convert sunlight directly into electricity. These panels have little impact on the environment and sunshine is free. The drawbacks are the large area needed to collect solar radiation at a useful rate, and the variable manner in which it arrives at the Earth's surface (clouds and fog can get in the way).

Solar energy can provide both warmth and electricity

Solar energy provides power for this building

Q How do we harness and use wind energy?

A Wind energy is harnessed using wind machines, highly advanced windmills made of high-strength materials. A typical wind machine stands as tall as a 20-story building and has blades 200 ft (60 m) across. Wind is collected in a wind farm, a cluster of dozens of machines scattered over a large area. Wind farms need a lot of land, but animals can graze around the machines. The most serious drawbacks may be the impact on wild bird populations and the visual impact on the landscape.

Q What is geothermal energy?

A The Earth's interior contains geothermal (heat) energy. At a geothermal power plant, water is pumped down into the Earth's crust, where the heat causes it to evaporate—making steam that turns turbines to produce electricity. Other kinds of plant use steam that emerges naturally from the Earth in the form of geysers. It is only possible to build geothermal plants where there are unique geological conditions. This form of energy makes very little impact on the environment.

Q How is biomass used to make electricity?

A When you throw another log on the fire, you are making heat using biomass energy—energy released from burning organic material including wood, straw, animal waste, garbage, and many other fuel sources. Utility companies are trying to develop ways to burn more biomass and less coal and natural gas to produce electricity. Some farmers grow burnable "energy crops" such as miscanthus grass.

Record Breakers

SOLAR POWER
Opened in 2012, the Gujarat PV Solar Park in India covers more than 3,000 acres (1,200 hectares) of desert and has a generating capacity of 600 MW (megawatts).

HYDROELECTRIC POWER
China's Three Gorges Dam across the Yangtze River is 7,660 ft (2,335 m) long and produces 22,000 MW of electricity.

WORLD'S SECOND LARGEST GEOTHERMAL PLANT
The Hellisheiði Power Station in Iceland is rated at 303 MW of electricity production.

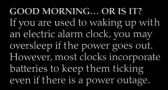

Life without electricity

YOU HAVE JUST READ a basic history of electricity, giving you a better understanding of this force and the important role it plays in our world. But what if the imaginary "plug" to the world's electricity supply were suddenly pulled? We all know how inconvenient life seems when the power is cut for just a few hours. Our daily lives have become so dependent on electricity it is hard to believe that people ever lived without it. On these pages we will follow a typical day without power from the electric company. Of course, to live completely without electricity, we'd have to eliminate batteries and telephones as well—but we'll allow them for purposes of this section.

GOOD MORNING... OR IS IT?
If you are used to waking up with an electric alarm clock, you may oversleep if the power goes out. However, most clocks incorporate batteries to keep them ticking even if there is a power outage.

SWITCHED ON
The first thing most people reach for when they get out of bed is the light switch. But if the light doesn't come on when the switch is flicked, there are alternatives. Every household should have a supply of battery-operated flashlights. The most powerful models give out a great amount of bright light.

GETTING READY FOR THE DAY
Without a power source, the whirr of the electric toothbrush and the whine of the hair dryer won't be heard. We can't even run water into our homes without an electric pump, which helps us draw water—so showering, washing, doing laundry, or flushing the toilet would be impossible.

BREAKFAST TIME
You might start your day by blending up a smoothie or reaching into the fridge for something to toast or microwave. Without electricity, however, none of the appliances you have come to rely on will be on the menu. Food in your refrigerator will stay fresh for only a while if there is a power cut.

Candles provide a source of light, but must be used with care in the home

UP IN THE AIR

Air travel is severely disrupted without electricity. During major blackouts, airports may close or divert flights, causing chaos that takes days to fix.

RED LIGHT, GREEN LIGHT

Although schools would probably close during a prolonged power outage, you'd have a difficult time getting there in the first place. Traffic lights would not function, leading to gridlock due to traffic jams on the streets.

ALL ABOARD?

Many forms of public transportation need electricity to keep people moving. City buses, subways, trams, and rail networks (such as Amtrak in the US, shown above) would be forced to suspend or severely curtail their services without electricity, leaving many would-be travelers out of luck.

COOL IT, HEAT IT

Without electricity to power air conditioning or central heating units, you would have to either open a window or light a fire for temperature control. In earlier times, people chose their home sites based on issues of heating and cooling. They looked for valleys that gave shelter from the elements and planted shady trees to keep the temperature down.

Dial-up Internet connections may work in power outages

HOME ENTERTAINMENT

Since going out during a power cut can be difficult, it may be best to stay at home. But how will you entertain yourself without the Internet, computer games, cable television, or music? Battery-operated music players and handheld computer games will keep you amused until the batteries run out. However, after that happens, you can always play a card or board game, tell each other stories, or even read a book!

MORNING NEWS

Before electricity, information traveled at a much slower pace. People visited each other to exchange news. Today, most of us are used to flipping on the morning news on the radio, television, or surfing the Internet to get the top stories and local weather and travel updates. Unless you have a battery- or crank-operated gadget in the house, however, a power failure will leave you in the dark.

Switching a phone off conserves its power

POWER DOWN

A home emergency kit would be helpful in case of a temporary power outage. Flashlights (with extra batteries) and candles can provide a source of light, and a battery-operated radio will keep you in touch with the outside world. Stock up with a first-aid kit as well as a nonelectric can opener, some nonperishable food and snacks, and plenty of drinking water.

ON THE PHONE

During a power outage, cordless telephones will not work. Cell phones, too, are only useful until their batteries run out—and that's assuming that their network is working. It's a good idea to keep a non-cordless phone in the house for emergencies.

Find out more

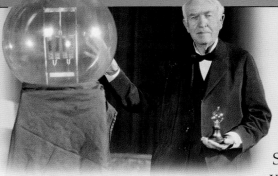

ELECTRICITY IS A FORCE THAT HAS TRANSFORMED the modern world. Here are some places to visit and things to do that will help you to understand why. Science museums contain plenty of exhibits to spark your knowledge about how electricity works. Many science centers feature fascinating hands-on exhibits that will enable you to experiment with electricity. Or, you can conduct simple experiments at home or at school. You might become the next Edison—if not, you can always visit his laboratory. Power plants, from your local plant to a huge megaplant, may offer guided tours that will show you how electricity is made.

THOMAS EDISON'S LABORATORY
In the early 1900s, a team of 200 scientists and engineers filled the laboratory of American inventor Thomas Edison (above). His lab and home, now part of the National Park Service in New Jersey, are now more likely to be bustling with tourists.

VISIT A SCIENCE MUSEUM
For the past two centuries, scientists and inventors have had many bright ideas about electricity. Science museums contain many artifacts related to our understanding of electricity, as well as examples of early electrical appliances, such as this electric kettle from the 1920s.

Cutaway of early electric kettle

Each hair repels the others. They stand on end to move as far away from each other as possible

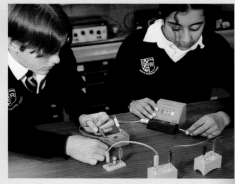

MAKE A SCIENCE PROJECT
With just a few batteries, buzzers, and bulbs (and some wire and paper clips to connect them), you can explore the wonders of electricity. Your local library is an excellent source of step-by-step project books, from simple circuits to more complex machines and motors.

USEFUL WEBSITES

www.eia.gov/kids
The interactive kid's page of the US Energy Information Administration.

www.energyhog.org
Fun activities help you explore and conserve energy.

www.energymatch.com/schoolhouse/kids
Interactive site dedicated to energy and electricity.

http://www.sparkmuseum.org/
Site of SPARK Museum of Electrical Invention.

VISIT A WORKING WONDER

Touring one of the massive dams constructed during the Great Depression in the United States (such as the Hoover Dam, shown here) provides visitors with an awe-inspiring learning experience. You will see the teams of gigantic turbines that generate electricity for millions of people, and find out how they work.

A large dam may have more than a dozen turbines

VISIT A WIND FARM

In some parts of the United States you can ride through a "forest" of towering silver windmills on a wind farm tour. Guides will show you the gigantic machines used to harness the power of the wind, and explain how this ancient method of capturing energy could help limit our dependence on fossil fuels in the future. Check the Internet or a travel guide for details.

VISIT A SCIENCE CENTER

Spending a day at an interactive science center will get you charged up about electricity. These centers help you learn more about the concepts in this book through fascinating hands-on experimentation. Here, two boys get an electrical charge when they touch a Van de Graaff generator.

Touching the generator gives you a positive charge

TOUR A POWER PLANT

Take a behind-the-scenes tour of your local power plant, and you will find out how the electricity you use is produced. Many non-nuclear power plants conduct tours for school and community groups. Check the Internet for details. Due to security concerns, most power plants will require advance reservations for tours.

Places to visit

EDISON NATIONAL HISTORIC SITE, WEST ORANGE, NJ
Visit Thomas Edison's restored laboratory and see the place where his inventions came to life.

NATIONAL INVENTORS HALL OF FAME MUSEUM, ALEXANDRIA, VA
Learn more about American inventors and how they profoundly changed everyday life.

EXPLORATORIUM, SAN FRANCISCO, CA
A unique museum that lets children learn about science and art through experimentation.

BOSTON MUSEUM OF SCIENCE, BOSTON, MA
Get high-voltage thrills at this museum's live Theater of Electricity show.

DISCOVERY PLACE KIDS MUSEUMS, HUNTERSVILLE, NC
One of several new Discovery Place KIDS locations across the region, appealing to families with young children.

NEW YORK HALL OF SCIENCE, FLUSHING, NY
Visit more than 400 exhibits in New York City's only interactive science and technology center.

ORLANDO SCIENCE CENTER, ORLANDO, FL
A state-of-the art science center that also offers fantastic camps and classes for kids.

THE FRANKLIN INSTITUTE, PHILADELPHIA, PA
Watch a bolt of lightning strike and have a hair-raising experience at this superb science center.

ST. LOUIS SCIENCE CENTER, ST. LOUIS, MO
This center features more than 700 hands-on exhibits for you to explore and enjoy.

NATIONAL MUSEUM OF NUCLEAR SCIENCE & HISTORY, ALBUQUERQUE, NM
Learn about the Atomic Age and how it has affected our lives, from atomic weapons to power plants and life-saving nuclear medicine.

Glossary

AMBER A hard fossil of tree gum or resin that is yellowish to brownish in color. The Greek word for amber, *elektron*, is the root of our word "electricity."

BATTERY A device that transforms chemical energy into electric energy. Originally, the term was applied to a group of two or more electric cells connected together. In common usage, the term "battery" now also applies to a single cell, such as the familiar household battery.

CAPACITOR A device that stores electrical energy using a positively charged surface and a negatively charged surface with a gap between them. The Leyden jar was an early form of capacitor. Capacitors were formerly called condensers.

CATHODE RAY TUBE Cathode rays are streams of high-speed electrons emitted from the heated cathode of a vacuum tube. In a cathode ray tube, the electrons are carefully directed into a beam. This beam is deflected by a magnetic field to scan the surface of a screen, which is lined with phosphorescent material. When the electrons hit this material, light is emitted. Cathode ray tubes were used in most televisions, computer displays, and video monitors.

CELL An electricity-making unit that delivers an electrical current as the result of a chemical reaction—a household battery, for example.

Cathode ray tube

CIRCUIT An electrical device that provides a path along which an electrical current can flow.

CONDENSER An old name for an electrical capacitor, now rarely used except in historical contexts.

CONDUCTOR Any material that allows electricity to move through it easily. Metals are especially good conductors.

CURRENT A measure of the flow of electrons moving past a certain point in a given time, usually through a metal wire or other conductor.

DIODE VALVE An electronic device with two electrodes or terminals that conducts current flow in only one direction. In the late 1950s, diode valves began to be replaced by transistors.

DYNAMO Another name for an electrical generator.

ELECTRIC CHARGE A measure of the excess or deficiency of electrons in a given object or material.

ELECTRICITY A form of energy produced by the flow of negatively and positively charged particles of matter.

ELECTROCARDIOGRAPH A medical instrument that records electric currents associated with contractions of the heart.

ELECTROLYSIS The process of breaking a chemical compound down into its elements by passing a direct current through it. Electrolysis of water, for example, produces hydrogen and oxygen.

ELECTROMAGNET A coil of wire, usually wound on an iron core, that produces a strong magnetic field when an electric current is sent through it.

ELECTRON A negatively charged particle; one of the three basic kinds of particles that make up an atom.

ELECTROPHORUS A simple electrostatic generator that generates repeated charges of static electricity.

ELECTROPLATING The process of coating an electroconductive material with a thin layer of metal by passing an electric current through the material.

ELECTROSCOPE A device used to measure the electric charge of an object or material.

ELECTROSTATIC ATTRACTION The attractive force between two oppositely charged ions.

FILAMENT BULB A type of incandescent lightbulb in which the light source is a fine electrical conductor heated by the passage of current.

FLUORESCENCE The emission of visible light by a substance, such as certain minerals, that is currently being exposed to ultraviolet light and absorbing radiation from it. The light appears in the form of glowing, distinctive colors.

GALVANOMETER An instrument used to measure small electric currents.

GENERATOR A machine that converts mechanical energy into electrical energy.

GEOTHERMAL ENERGY Energy derived from the internal heat of the Earth that can be used to generate electricity.

HEATING ELEMENT The part of a heater or stove that transforms fuel or electricity into heat.

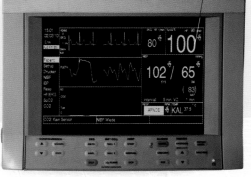

The display shows heart rate and blood pressure

Electrocardiograph machine

HYDROELECTRIC Refers to the process of using flowing water to create electricity.

INDUCTION The process of producing a magnetic charge through changes in an electric current flow.

INDUCTION COIL A coil for producing high voltage from a low-voltage source. It consists of a primary coil through which the direct current flows, an interrupter, and a secondary coil with more turns in which the high voltage is induced.

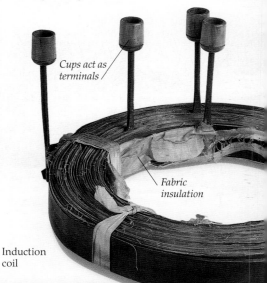

Cups act as terminals

Fabric insulation

Induction coil

Leyden jar

INDUCTION MOTOR The simplest type of electric motor; converts electrical energy into mechanical energy using a rotating magnetic field.

INSULATOR A material that resists the flow of electric current.

LEYDEN JAR A glass jar or bottle used to accumulate electricity. Coated with foil both inside and out, it is connected to a metal conducting rod that passes through an insulating stopper and charges the jar with electricity.

MAGNETISM A property, possessed by certain materials, that attracts or repels similar materials. Magnetism is closely associated with moving electricity.

METER A device used to measure electricity consumption in a business or home.

MORSE CODE A communications system of letters coded into dots and dashes, sent as short electrical signals (dots) and long signals (dashes) along a telegraph line.

MOTOR A machine that converts electrical energy into mechanical energy.

PACEMAKER An electronic device that is surgically implanted into the heart and chest in order to control the heart's rhythm when it beats erratically.

PHOTOVOLTAIC CELL An electronic device that converts light into electricity.

POWER PLANT An electrical generating plant that sends energy directly into homes, offices, and factories.

POWER TOWER A large steel structure that supports high-tension power lines.

RADIO The wireless transmission and reception of electric impulses or signals by means of electromagnetic waves.

RESISTANCE A material's opposition to the flow of electric current.

SCANNER An electrical device that makes an image of or records an object using a moving beam, line by line.

SELENIUM A light-sensitive element that occurs naturally in food and soils and that generates electric current when exposed to light.

SILICON CHIP A wafer-thin slice of silicon that contains thousands of microscopic electronic circuits.

SOLAR POWER Sunlight that has been converted into thermal or electrical energy.

SPARK A short electrical discharge between two conductors.

STATIC ELECTRICITY An electrical charge that builds up due to friction between two dissimilar materials. Friction removes some electrons from one object and deposits them on the other.

STEP-DOWN TRANSFORMER A transformer that reduces voltage.

TELEGRAPH A mechanical or electrical apparatus used to communicate at a distance over a wire, usually through Morse code.

TELEPHONE An instrument used for voice communication that works by converting sound waves into electrical energy, and electrical energy into sound waves.

TELEVISION A form of communication that operates through the transmission of pictures and sounds in the form of electrical waves.

THERMOCOUPLE A device that produces a small voltage that indicates a temperature difference between two metals.

TIDAL POWER Power obtained by the generation of electricity using changing ocean tides.

TRANSFORMER A device that changes electricity from one voltage to another.

TRANSISTOR A tiny electrical device used to amplify an electrical signal that can be switched on and off to either aid or inhibit the flow of electrical current.

Water drives a massive turbine

Telegraph

TURBINE A device for converting the flow of a fluid (air, steam, water, or hot gases) into mechanical motion that in turn can be used to produce electricity.

VERSORIUM The earliest form of scientific electroscope, created by William Gilbert in 1600. Used to indicate the direction of an electronic force, the device consisted simply of a light metallic needle balanced on a pivot, similar to a compass.

VOLT A unit of electrical pressure that measures the force or push of electricity.

VOLTAIC PILE A device that uses different metals, separated by moist chemicals, to produce a flow of electric charge; a form of battery.

WATT A unit of electrical power used to indicate the rate of energy produced or consumed by an electrical device. One watt is equal to one joule of energy per second. The watt is named for James Watt, inventor of the modern steam engine.

XEROGRAPHY MACHINE Another name for the electrostatic printer, invented by Chester Carlson in 1938.

Index

A

accumulators 19
Adams, George 10
air filters 15
alkaline cells 18
alternating current 12, 36, 40, 41
alternators 40
amber 6, 8, 14
ammeters 24
Ampère, André-Marie 26, 27
amplifiers 34, 53, 61, 63
amps 24, 27, 42
animals
  electricity in 7, 16, 64
  subduing 50
anodes 18, 19, 33, 54
antennas 60, 61
appliances, domestic 48–49, 66–67
armatures 37, 39, 40, 42
atoms 12, 20, 31, 54

B

Baird, John Logie 62
bakelite 21
Barlow, Peter 38
batteries 12, 16–19, 20, 24, 26, 64
Becquerel, Antoine 47
Bell, Alexander Graham 58
biomass 45, 64, 65
Bluetooth 61
Brown repeaters 59

C

capacitors 9, 12–13
carbon arc lamps 32, 37, 43
Carlisle, Anthony 32
Carlson, Chester 14
cathode ray tubes 62–63
cathode rays 54–55
cathodes 18, 19, 33
Cavendish, Henry 20
cell phones 61, 67
cells 16, 18, 19, 20, 24, 53
ceramic insulators 21, 47
circuits 20, 24, 34, 48
Clarke, Edward 36
Cockcroft-Walton generator 12
coffee makers 49
coherers 57

communications 56–63, 67
commutators 36, 37, 39, 41
computers 61, 64, 67
conductors 8, 10, 20–21, 22, 23, 34, 52
Cooke, William 56
cooking 48
Coulomb, Charles de 11, 23
Crookes, William 54
crystals 52, 53
Curie, Pierre and Jacques 53
currents, flowing 25

D

Daniell, John 19
Davenport, Thomas 38
Davy, Humphrey 19, 32
De Forest, Lee 55, 61
diode valves 63
direct current 12, 37, 40
disk generators 35
distribution networks 42–45
doorbells 30
dry cells 18
dynamos 36, 37, 38, 40, 42, 43

E

Edison, Thomas 39, 41, 43, 46, 47, 54, 55, 58, 68
Einthoven, Willem 51
electro-medical machines 50–51
electrocardiographs 7, 51
electrochemical reactions 16, 18–19
electrocution 50, 64
electrodes 18, 19, 33
electrodynamics 27
electrolysis 19, 32–33, 46
electrolytes 18, 19, 33
electromagnetic field theory 34, 60–61
electromagnetic induction 29, 34, 40, 58
electromagnetic waves 60–61
electromagnetism 26, 27, 28–31, 57
electromotive force 34, 35
electrons 20, 52, 54, 55, 62, 63
electrophorus 16, 17
electrophotography 14
electroplating 32, 33, 36, 42
electroscopes 11, 21
electrostatic charge 10, 12, 50, 53
  using 14–15
energy 24, 44–45

F

Faraday, Michael 28, 32, 34–35, 36, 38, 40
farads 13
Ferranti, Sebastian 44
filament bulbs 47
fires, electric 49
Fleming's tubes 55, 63
flowing currents 25
fluorescence 47
food mixers 49
fossil fuels 44, 45, 65
Franklin, Benjamin 7, 8, 64

G

Galvani, Luigi 16, 24, 50
galvanometers 24, 34, 35, 53
generators 10, 12, 30, 34, 35, 36, 40, 41, 42, 43, 44, 64
geothermal energy 45, 65
Gilbert, William 8
Gramme, Z. T. 37
Gramme dynamos 37
Gray, Stephen 10

H

Hauksbee, Francis 10
heating, domestic 49, 67
heating elements 49
henries 35
Henry, Joseph 28, 29, 30, 34–35, 36, 58
Hertz, Heinrich 57, 60
high-tension batteries 19
homes, electricity in 46–49
horse power 43
household current 48
Hubble Telescope 53
hydroelectricity 44, 45, 65, 69

IJK

iconoscopes 63
incandescent bulbs 42, 43, 47
induction 9, 11, 29, 34, 35
  coil 34–35, 40, 60
  motor 41
  ring 35
insulators 20, 21
integrated circuits 63
Internet 61, 67
inverse square law 11
irons 48
Joule, James 24

joules 24
kettles 49, 68
kilowatt-hours 46

L

Large Hadron Collider 31
lead-acid batteries 19
Leclanché, Georges 18
left-hand rule 27
Leyden jars 8, 9, 12, 13
lifting power 28, 29
lightbulbs 19, 46, 47
light rays 60
lighthouses 36, 37, 61
lighting 19, 36, 37, 41, 43
lightning 6, 7, 12
  conductors 8, 10
long-life cells 18
loudspeakers 53, 61
low-energy bulbs 47, 64

M

magnetism 6, 7, 26–31, 34–35
magneto-electric machines 36–37
Marconi, Guglielmo 55, 57, 60–61
Maxwell, James Clerk 60
measurement 24–25, 46
medicine 30, 36, 50–51
meters, electricity 46
meters, flow 25
microphones 58, 59
Morse, Samuel 57
Morse code 31, 57, 61
motors, electric 27, 30, 38–39, 41, 43
movement 38–39
museums 68–69

NO

nerves 6, 7, 16, 50
Nicholson, William 32
Nobili, Leopold 24
nuclear power 44, 65
Oersted, Hans Christian 26, 27, 38
Ohm, Georg 22, 23
ohms 23
oscillating electric charge 60

P

pacemakers 51
Parsons, Charles 42
particle accelerators 12, 30, 31
Peltier, Jean 52

pens, electric 39
photocopying 14–15
photoelectric effect 52–53
photovoltaic effect 53, 62
piezoelectric effect 52–53
Pixii, Hippolyte 36
Planté, Gaston 18
plugs 21
porcelain insulators 21
potassium 19, 32
potential difference 22
power cuts 66–67
power lines 21, 45, 64
power plants 41, 44–45, 65, 69
Priestley, Joseph 10

R

radio 13, 19, 61
  waves 57, 60–61, 62, 63
radioactivity 47
receivers 31, 57, 58–59, 61, 62
renewable energy 45, 64, 65
resinous electricity 8
resistance 22–23, 24, 25
resistors 23
rheostats 22
Richmann, Georg 8
right-hand rule 34
Rutherford, Ernest 54

S

scanners 62, 63
Seebeck, Thomas 52
Seebeck effect 52, 53
selenium 14, 15
self-inductance 35
sewing machines 39
Siemens, Werner von 37
Siemens company 39
silicon chips 63, 64
Singer, Isaac 39
solar power 44, 45, 65
solenoids 30, 31
sound waves 58–59, 61
space technology 53, 64
sparks 8, 9, 10, 12
spectroscopy 54
starter motors 31
static electricity 7, 9
stators 41
steam power 42
Steinmetz, Charles 40
step-down/up transformers 41, 44–45
stereophonic sound 53
stock tickers 43
street lighting 43
Sturgeon, William 28, 30
subatomic particles 55

T

telegraphy 18, 23, 24, 26, 29, 31, 56–57, 58
telephones 30, 58–9, 67
television 54, 62–63, 67
Tesla, Nikola 40, 41
Thales of Miletus 6
thermionic valves 55
thermocouples 23, 52–53
thermoelectricity 52–53
thermometers 52, 53
Thomson, Joseph John 54, 55
tidal power 45
torsion balance 11
towers 45
trains 39, 56
transformers 30, 40–41, 61
transistors 63
transmitters 57, 58–59, 62
transportation 67
triode valves 61
turbines 42–43, 44

UV

ultraviolet light 47
vacuum tubes 55, 63
valves 55, 61, 63
Van de Graaff, Robert 12
Van de Graaff generators 12, 69
variable capacitors 13, 62
versorium 8
vitreous electricity 8
Volta, Alessandro 16, 17, 26, 32
voltaic pile 16–17, 32
voltameters 32–3
volts 17, 18, 19, 20, 22, 23, 42, 44

WXZ

Watson, Thomas 58
Watt, James 42
watts 42, 46
websites 68
Wheatstone, Charles 56
Wimshurst, James 9
Wimshurst machine 8–9
wind energy 45, 65, 69
wireless 57, 60–61, 62
xerography 14
Zworykin, Vladimir 63

Acknowledgments

The publisher would like to thank:
Fred Archer, Brian Bowers, Roger Bridgman, Janet Carding, Eryl Davies, Robert Excell, Graeme Fyffe, Derek Hudson, Dr. Ghislaine Lawrence, Barry Marshall and the staff of the Museum Workshop, Douglas Millard, Victoria Smith, Peter Stephens, Peter Tomlinson, Kenneth Waterman, Anthony Wilson, and David Woodcock for advice and help with the provision of objects for photography at the Science Museum; Dave Mancini at Nortech and Peter Griffiths for the model making; Deborah Rhodes for page makeup; Peter Cooling for computer artwork; Robert Hulse for standing in for Michael Faraday and Humphry Davy; Karl Adamson and Tim Ridley for assistance with the photography; Jack Challoner for help in the initial stages of the book; Monica Byles for proofreading; and Helen Peters for indexing.

Picture research Deborah Pownall and Catherine O'Rourke
Illustrations Kuo Kang Chen
Picture credits

(Key: a-above; b-below/bottom; c-center; f-far; l-left; r-right; t-top)
Ashmolean Museum, Oxford 8tr.
Bildarchiv Preussischer Kulturbesitz 40br.
Bridgeman Art Library 8bc; /Philips 32tl.
Bt Museum, London 8c; 58bl.
Hulton Picture Co. /Bettmann Archive 14tc; 16bc; 28tl; /Bettmann Archive 52tr; 56cl; 57br; 58cl; 58tl; 61tl; 62cl; /Bettmann Archive 63cr.
Getty Images: H. Armstrong Roberts / Retrofile 58crb; Encyclopaedia Britannica / Universal Images Group 51br, Science & Society Picture Library 21bl, 36clb, Kenzo Tribouillard / AFP 45cra.
Patsy Kelly 12–13.
Kobal Collection 12bl; 50cl.
Mansell Collection 6cl; 24cl; 47cr.
Mary Evans Picture Library 7cl; 15bl; 19tc; 19c; 27cl; 30tr; 37cl; 41tr; 43tr; 44bl; 46tl; 46bl; 49cr; 61tr.
MIT Museum, Cambridge, Massachusetts 12c.
National Portrait Gallery, London 10tr.
National Portrait Gallery, Washington 29tr.
NEI Parsons 42cr; 43bl.

Ann Ronan Picture Library 11tc; 19cb; 42tl; 51tr; 53tl.
Rover Group 33br.
Royal Institution, London 35tr; 35cr.
Science Museum Photo Library cover front tl; back tl; 9tr; 18tl; 23tl; 27clb; 29br; 34tl; 41tc; 48tr; 55cr; 57tr; 60clb.
Science Photo Library /Gordon Garrado cover front c; 7tr; /Simon Fraser 7cr; /David Parker 12bc; 29bl; /David Parker 31br; / Jean-Loup Charmet 43tc; /Hank Morgan 45tr; /Gary Ladd 45crb; 52bl; 53br; / Jean-Loup Charmet 54bl. Wellcome Institute Library 24crb.
Zefa 41br.
Alamy: Photofusion Picture Library 71tr
Corbis: Anamitra Chakladar / Demotix 31br; Paul Souders 7br; Jochen Tack / imagebroker 7cr; Paul Almasy 65br; Lester V. Bergman 68br; Bettman Collection 64tr, 68tl; PITCHAL FREDERIC 69bcr; Charles Gupton 69c; Eric and David Hosking 64br; Gunter Marx Photography 68tl; Sally A. Morgan; Ecoscene 65tr; Joseph Sohm ctl Getty Images: AFP 68br; National Geographic 69cr

Chrissy McIntyre: 68cl Science Photo Library/ Photo Researchers: 68bl

Jacket images: Front: Dorling Kindersley: Phil Farrand ca, The Science Museum, London tr, tc, tc/ (Phone); Science Photo Library: Steve Allen b; Back: Dorling Kindersley: The Science Museum, London cr, cb, tl

With the exception of the items listed above, and the objects on pages 6, 22, 25, 31c, 33t, 49c, 52, 53t, all the photographs in this book are of objects in the collections of the Science Museum, London.

Wall chart: Corbis: Radius Images bl; Dorling Kindersley: ESA tr, The Science Museum, London c, cl, cra, cr, cb, cl/ (thermocouple), clb, bc; Getty Images: Encyclopedia Britannica / Universal Images Group crb, DaveArnoldPhoto.com / Flickr tl

All other images © Dorling Kindersley
For further information see:
www.dkimages.com